The Project Saboteur

Knowing Him is Just the Beginning

Jeroen Gietema *&* Dion Kotteman

Claret Press

CLARET PRESS

Copyright © 2019 Jeroen Gietema and Dion Kotteman
The moral right of the author has been asserted.

Cover design and typesetting by Ginny Wood
Illustrations by Peter Koch at peterkoch.nl

ISBN paperback: 978-1-910461-42-6
ISBN ebook: 978-1-910461-43-3

This ebook and paperback can be ordered from all bookstores as well as from Amazon and other eplatforms. The ebook can be ordered from eplatforms such as Amazon and iBook among others.

A CIP catalogue record for this book is available from the British Library.

www.claretpress.com

Table of Contents

About the Authors

Dion Kotteman is a well-recognised and established speaker and advisor. As an independent executive strategist he advises many companies and organisations. Previously he was the Chief Information Officer of the Dutch Government. He now runs his own company.

His working history includes: general manager of the Dutch National Audit Authority, and executive in the banking world, mainly in IT and security. He has an extensive executive project management experience within several financial institutions. He is a non-executive member of the board of an insurance company.

He also worked for Interpol and Europol, was CIO of the Dutch Criminal Intelligence Service, and of the Dutch State Police. He acted as chairman of many Netherlands EU governmental delegations and projects on security and data exchange.

He holds an executive master of business administration of Nyenrode University, the Netherlands, and of the Wharton Business School, Pennsylvania University, USA. He publishes and lectures on the subject of project management and IT. His books are published in several European countries.

www.dionkotteman.com

info@dionkotteman.com

Jeroen Gietema is a leading project and programme manager, heading up large international ICT programs. With more than 30 years experience in financial, governmental, industrial and logistic organisations, he has in the last decade, built extensive know-how in Agile development of complex software solutions at scale.

After studying computer technique and business science, Jeroen worked for Volmac and Capgemini. With Capgemini, he worked as Project Manager and Deputy Area Quality Manager

Jeroen is now co-owner and CEO of Cedira BV, a company that develops and provides WEB based solutions and management consulting services. Two solutions Cedira developed are Chef99.nl, an affiliate marketing platform, and ProSpondo, an assessment and impact analyses engine with advanced and unique analysis and reporting capabilities.

www.cedira.com

j.gietema@cedira.com

Based on their extensive experience in getting projects to succeed, Jeroen Gietema and Dion Kotteman wrote *The Project Saboteur* and *The Project Saboteur and* PRINCE2. *The Project Saboteur* is available in Dutch, German and English. They are regularly invited to give lectures about the human factor on project failure. They explain how to recognise saboteurs as well as how to implement effective defence mechanisms.

www.projectsaboteur.com

info@projectsaboteur.com

Acknowledgements

Joop Swieringa agreed to comment on a draft version of the book, and that has contributed to its quality. Our sincere thanks. Paula Steenwinkel, of Tekstformule, agreed to check the original Dutch, and this had the same result. Many thanks to her as well. Peter Koch produced the illustrations. Thank you. Jonathan Ellis translated it to English. Thanks pal! Dave Tomkins added a British perspective to the book: thanks! Katie Isbester of Claret Press edited the British edition and we are very grateful for the improvements she has made.

Most of all we would like to thank many, many people who served as perfect project saboteurs. They provided us with enough examples to fill this book. They gave the empirical data to make this book possible, whether it was in Germany, in the Netherlands, in the UK, or in Switzerland. And it still continues.

And our utmost gratitude of course goes to all those organisations that spent such a nice tuition fee on failing projects! Without those projects we would not have been able to write this book.

And of course we're not going to thank our wives for their patience; we want to thank them for their never ending love.

Jeroen Gietema & Dion Kotteman
Nieuwegein and The Hague, March 2019

Foreword

On March 4, 1921, Warren Gamaliel Harding became the 29th President of the United States. If remembered at all, Harding is remembered for the first major presidential scandal, known as Teapot Dome. The Teapot Dome was a scandal involving Harding's Secretary of the Interior, Albert Fall. Fall did a secret leasing deal for federal oil reserves and got kickbacks from Sinclair Oil. Harding was slow to take action and let Congress do most of the investigation, which ultimately led to Fall's conviction. In response to the scandal, Harding is reported to have made these immortal remarks: "I have no trouble with my enemies, but my damn friends, they're the ones that keep me walking the floor nights!"

Projects in general and software projects in particular are all about change. Change will have an impact on different people in different ways. Change also causes fear and uncertainty. It is a rare project that does not have detractors. Dion Kotteman and Jeroen Gietema's Project Saboteur provides insight into how some people may react to changes they perceive as unfavorable to their position and place. In most cases people will act in their own self-interest and preservation. This book will help you make decisions through understanding their behavior and motivation. Project managers can use this new understanding to help in the control and management of the project. Executive sponsors will find helpful hints for neutralizing or transforming the project saboteur to help move the project forward.

A Roman gladiator's purpose was to fight well in hopes of either beating his opponent or gaining a reprieve to fight another day. In most cases the combatants were set up so that each had a different advantage either for close combat or a distant struggle to make the fight more interesting and show off the latest martial arts. Each gladiator clearly knew his opponent. Bob Kelley, serial CIO, related an ERP systems project that had its own gladiator. There was one woman in purchasing who openly refused to help with the implementation and she put up a fight. She went so far as to poison the well for the other people. The organization gave her the thumbs down and helped her retire with a nice severance package. Unfortunately, project saboteurs are not always so aboveboard. They exhibit a more passive-aggressive appoach. They are more likely to give you a bear hug before stabbing you in the back.

The first thing you need to do is recognize the project saboteur. This book helps you recognize the habits and behaviors of a potential saboteur. Once you recognize a project saboteur, managing her or him is crucial to the project. The big takeaways from this book are the tools to be able to deal with the potential saboteur without hurting the project or your career. This book is both fun to read and insightful. However, you will no longer look at the people in the project meeting in the same way, but you will have the awareness to not be blindsided by the project saboteur. You need to keep your enemies close, but your friends closer. Hopefully you will not be walking the floor nights.

Jim Johnson
Dreamer
The Standish Group

Introduction

It's just not fair. There are plenty of books about how to carry out projects brilliantly, but there are no books about destroying them underhandedly — although projects are constantly and intentionally doomed to oblivion.

It is about time that the project saboteurs were given the proper tool: a book that explains how you can destroy a project.

It is not easy to leave the well-trodden path. Much of the advice given in the world of management – but also elsewhere — seems intent on keeping you on the straight and narrow. That is hardly surprising; after all, the world will be better for it.

Only when we leave the well-trodden path do we see things that remain hidden from others, and only then do we discover a new perspective on an age-old theme. Only then do we realise that it is well worth describing how to undermine a project — and how extremely educational that is. Educational not only for the saboteur, but also for you, to arm yourself against these saboteurs and their undermining actions.

> *"Look like th' innocent flower, but be the serpent under 't"*
>
> Shakespeare, Macbeth Act 1, scene 5

This book begins with the introduction to the project saboteur, his motives and his approaches. Or her motives and approaches. Because if there's one place where there's gender equity, it's in sabotage and counter-sabotage. For the sake of ease, let's say they're all men: the saboteurs, their victims and the well-armed counter-saboteurs (even though they're not!). The book then continues by placing the director, the project manager, the user, the specialist and the member of the Joint Consultative Committee in the role of project saboteur. The book ends with a conspiracy in which the saboteurs form a criminal organisation in order to torpedo a project. To show how project saboteurs practice their undermining activities in real life we enriched the book with a number of cases based on true facts; to protect those successful saboteurs we provided them with new names and new sceneries to perform their hideous acts.

You might get the idea that sabotage is everywhere and nothing can be done about it. The first is true, but the second isn't. You can certainly do something about this. The main goal of this book is to make you aware of this phenomenon called project sabotage. It is there, believe us. To help you in your battle against these saboteurs, we end each chapter with a section on how to recognise the saboteur and prevent him from being successful. You can read these sections separately; it will give you a clear approach of how to prevent project failure due to project sabotage. That should make life easier!

Finally, based on some interesting publications, we challenge the commonly accepted causes for project failure. By analysing publications, concerning several failed projects, it becomes clear that the human factor is an important reason why these projects failed. But, funny enough, not recognised as such.

Look at this:
Was it so hard to build a new airport in Berlin, the Brandenburger Airport? It had an overrun of billions. (www.berlin-airport.de)

Was it not possible to give MI5 a proper record management system? (*The Independent* May 12th 2013).

The BBC has scrapped a £98m digital production system, which its director general said had "wasted a huge amount of licence fee payers' money". The Digital Media Initiative was set up in 2008 but was halted last autumn having never become fully operational. Mrs Hodge (chair of the House of Commons Public Accounts Committee) described the episode as 'a terrible shock and clearly completely shambolic'. (BBC News Site, 22651126)

Europe does not have the monopoly on project failure. According to the 2015 Standish CHAOS report, the overall project success rate in North America was only 31% with 18% of the projects failing completely.

It's about time to look into the real reason of project failure.

1 | The project saboteur

Each project has its opponents. Everybody knows them — people who, for one reason or another, have a self-interest in having a project fail. But these opponents are often amateurs. They just mess around. Do they know the best way to attack a project in a properly structured way? No, of course they don't! There are courses for project managers, but there's nothing similar for project saboteurs. The saboteurs have to do it as they see fit; there is absolutely no support for amateur saboteurs who want to become true professionals. This book redresses the balance, by explaining how you can undermine a project efficiently, effectively, but most importantly, professionally. Not by occasionally saying you disagree, but working in a subtle, thorough and irresistible way on the destruction of the project. Not empty words, but planned action. The idea that planning is somehow reserved to the project manager is nonsense. Effective subversive action needs good planning. And the plan must be professionally implemented. That's what this book is about.

Why would anybody want to undermine a project?

Some project saboteurs are convinced that the project is bad for the company and they will do anything to protect the company from making a mistake. Others believe that if the project fails, employment will be protected.

And there are other, less noble motives: the failure of a project offers the saboteur the chance of improving his position or of encouraging people to move on to other things: generally by beating a hasty retreat by the back door.

The dominant motive is survival; a budding saboteur comes to the conclusion that the project could result in him losing his job. And he's not going to let that happen. He has to put up some resistance, otherwise who will pay for his car, his mortgage and his children's education? He, so obviously indispensible, is in danger of becoming superfluous.

"Food is the first thing, morals follow on"

B. Brecht: The Threepenny Opera
Ballad on the question: What Keeps Mankind Alive?

It's about time that this important player, the project saboteur, is provided with professional tools that will allow him to successfully undermine any project he wishes.

In essence, a project is extremely simple, and so, too, is its destruction. Many trainers and organisations that supply expensive project managers are not likely to agree with this. In project management training, people succeed in portraying projects as exceptionally complex, when in fact they are really fairly simple. There is a director, who states that a certain result (a change or a product) is necessary. Then there is a project manager, who brings the assignment to a successful conclusion within the time and budget allocated. He draws up a plan for this and hires specialists. The project manager asks the users what they would like to have and whether they can work with the result. Now and again, he reports the progress of the project to the director. The agreed result is delivered and accepted by the director. And that's it.

In his efforts to undermine the project, the professional project saboteur makes use of the very elements that the project manager should use to keep it under control: assignment, plan, reporting and result.

The project saboteur has it a lot easier than the project manager; the saboteur knows the project manager, but the project manager does not know who the saboteur is. The project manager must report and communicate verifiable facts; the project saboteur need only insinuate suspicions.

It will by now be clear that the project saboteur has purely human motives for committing his deed. We need only refer to Maslow and his behavioural pyramid. See Appendix B for more information on Maslow's hierarchy of needs.

Motivation, however, is not enough for bringing about the failure of a project; there must also be opportunities. The saboteur must have formal or informal influence. Or both. Formal influence is something you derive from your position. Informal influence is derived from your knowledge or social position.

If, for example, the saboteur is the manager of the department for which the project result is intended, then there is a good chance that he is the person responsible for accepting the result. This is an ideal position from which to frustrate both the demands placed on the project result and the acceptance of it. If the saboteur is an expert or a specialist, he not only has possibilities for questioning the proposed solutions but also for combating the actual need for the project. If, as a result of his knowledge as a specialist, he ends up in the project team, his possibilities are virtually endless.

Even if his influence is not based on knowledge or hierarchy, the saboteur can still bring about the downfall of a project. To do this, he needs an informal access to the formal project network. He must be able to influence the formal process. He can acquire this position by cozying up to the real players in the process, creating bonds of trust and friendship. After all, friends do not doubt each others' motives and always take each other seriously.

Intake of the project saboteur

Would you like to know whether you have what it takes to be a saboteur, whether you have the motives and the possibilities to make a project fall flat on its face? Then you should take the following self-assessment.

Question	Answer	Yes points	Score potential saboteur
Have I the proper motives?			
If the project succeeds	No problem	0	
	I'll probably lose my job	3	
	My career will come to a dead end	2	
	I'll take over from my boss	0	
If the project fails	No problem	2	
	I'll probably lose my job	0	
	I'll keep my position in the company	3	
	The company will go bankrupt within a year	0	
	I'll take over from my boss	2	
If I lose my job	I can quickly find a job with another company	0	
	I'm too old to be considered for a job with another company	2	
	I do not have the qualifications to get a job with another company	2	
	I will have to sell my house	2	
	I will lose the respect of my partner	2	
	I will lose the respect of my family and friends	2	
If my career comes to a dead end in the company	I'll lose my influence	1	
	I will lose the respect of my partner	1	
	I will lose the respect of my family and friends	1	
Do I have the right mentality (Conscience)?			
It doesn't bother me	If a colleague is fired	2	
	If a colleague is falsely blamed	2	
	To tell a lie to my own advantage	2	
	To manipulate reports to my own advantage	2	
	To manipulate reports to the disadvantage of a colleague	2	
	If I am the cause of a colleague being fired	2	
	Using somebody else to carry out my actions so that I keep out of the firing line	2	
I am proud	If I am rewarded for a colleague's idea	1	
	If I can blame a colleague for my own failings	1	
	If a colleague passes off my idea as his own	-2	

Question	Answer	Yes points	Score potential saboteur
Do I have sufficient influence in the organisation?			
People consider me	A specialist	1	
	A do-er	0	
	Somebody to fetch the coffee	0	
	A manager	1	
	Needy?	1	
The following statement applies to me	People listen to me	2	
	My ideas are often adopted	2	
	People don't often take me seriously	0	
	I am trusted by people on the work floor	2	
	The board of management takes me into its confidence	2	
	My boss regularly asks me for my opinion	2	
	My colleagues eagerly follow my advice	2	
	I have a lot of informal contacts	2	
Do I have sufficient knowledge?			
The following statement applies to me	I fully understand the company processes	1	
	I know my colleagues' quality	1	
	I know who has what influence within the organisation	2	
	I know the preferences and aversions of the most important people in the organisation	2	
Project approach	I understand the way projects are run	2	
	I can and will make the project process my own	1	
	I know what the requirements/acceptance criteria are	2	
	I know what the role of project manager entails	1	
Am I up for it?			
Do I want the project to fail?	No	-30	
	Yes - and I'm going to see it does	30	
	Yes, but I've no time to see that it does	-30	
TOTAL (maximum 100)			

If you scored more than 70 points then you have passed your entrance exam as 'project saboteur'. This book is a must for you. If you scored less, then reading this book will help you recognise your undermining friends and colleagues, and arm yourself against them.

How to identify the project saboteur

If not the failure but the success of the project is your goal, it is worthwhile to analyse if it is in someone's interest to manipulate your project. Is this often done? No! Is this difficult? Not really.

By wrapping the 'intake of the project saboteur' questionnaire in the frame work of the stakeholder analysis you own the perfect instrument to investigate which of your potential project opponents are likely to take action against the project success.

Each stakeholder analysis starts by determining the position of the stakeholders in the spectrum from Supporter to Opponent. After identifying the position of the stakeholders you apply the questionnaire per stakeholder.

Only if the stakeholder has the right motivation, the competence, and also the opportunity to manipulate a project, is it to be expected that he will take action to undermine the project's results.

As the position of your stakeholders might change during the course of the project, it is wise to regularly renew the project manipulation stakeholder analysis.

In the chapters regarding the players, we give you the preventive measures.

IT Project success and failure in 2015

The Standish group reported on project results in 2015. 25.000 projects were assessed against the resolution definition: OnTime, OnBuget and satisfactory result.

The IT Project success rate as presented in this report is rather low: in 2015 only 29% of the software development projects were considered to be successful, meaning that these projects delivered OnTime, OnBudget, with a satisfactory result. 52% of the projects were listed with the qualification challenged and 19% failed completely. What is even more amazing is that the project success rate doesn't show any improvement over the years. In 2011 too 29% of the projects were considered to be successful and 22% of the projects failed.

Let's combine the Standish CHAOS figures with some Gartner publications.

According to Gartner in 2015 $3.5 trillion will be spent on IT worldwide. Approximately 19% is spent on change. This represents an amount of approximately $665 billion spend worldwide on IT projects. The logical conclusion is that $126 billion of this amount goes down the drain each year due to project failure. If you add to this amount to the inefficiency costs of challenged projects we assume that the sum lost on projects each year is in the order of magnitude of least $300 billion.

Software development projects are clearly in chaos, and we can no longer imitate the three monkeys: hear no failures, see no failures, speak no failures!

Of course, the Standish figures have been challenged here and there, but there is overwhelming proof that projects are not as successful as we want them to be.

Want to know the underlying causes and what we can do to improve?

Continue reading this book!.

Sources used: Standish group Chaos report 2015; Transforming the business - Gartner 2003; Worldwide IT Spending Forecast – Gartner 2015

2 | Use CRIME1 as a weapon against PRINCE2

A professional project manager has his tools: PRINCE2[1] for example, a structured method of achieving a project result. There is not, as yet, a professional method for undermining a project. Until now. We are introducing CRIME1 as an anti-PRINCE2 weapon.

Sabotage is more successful if you do it in a structured way. As project saboteur, you must know which instruments can best be deployed in which stage of the project. The following illustration shows where a project saboteur has to intervene in the project management and with what:

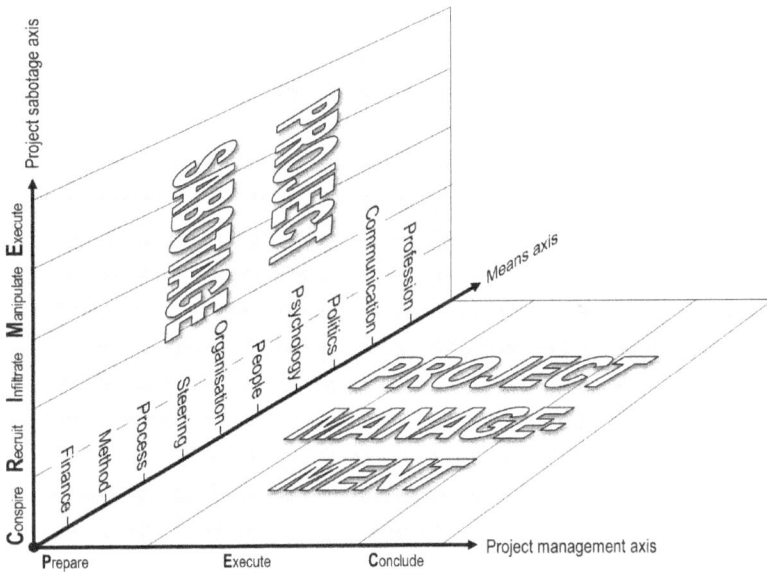

---

[1] The PRINCE2 method (projects in controlled environments) is a much used method for project execution

The project management axis indicates how the *project manager* directs the project structurally using, for example, PRINCE2 and represents the success of the project.

The project undermining axis indicates how the project saboteur disrupts the project using the CRIME method. This axis represents the success of the *project saboteur*.

The means axis indicates which means the project saboteur has at his disposal for purposely doing in a project. It will not surprise you that these are the same means that the project manager uses to keep the project on the right track. Compare it to a burglar robbing a jewellery story under the cover of darkness. At night, the jeweller puts his jewellery in a safe and turns on the alarm. If the burglar is to get his hands on those jewels, he must turn off the same alarm and open the same safe.

The CRIME1 method is an approach that targets the destruction of a project. If you wish to plan an attack, you should preferably take the follow steps:

Conspire Preparation must be done: pinpoint the decision-makers and ascertain where the formal and informal power lies.

- Why do people want this project?

- What problems do they think it will solve?

- What is the objective?

- How much is it worth to the decision-maker?

- Decide which area you will concentrate on in order to have the project fail by asking yourself:

- Which means will you use at which stage?

- Which weapons will you deploy when?

- Whom you can influence: the specialists, the decision-makers, the users, the opponents and the colleagues.

- What stage is the project in?

In short: plan thoroughly.

Recruit This is the first operational stage of CRIME1. You have mapped all the people involved, determined what influence they have and which of them can be influenced. Now you approach them and deploy them.

Infiltrate Make sure you become a participant in the project. You can act much more effectively as a participant than as an onlooker. Influence the doubters, the specialists, and the users. Do not be afraid of causing casualties, but remain safely out of range.

Manipulate In this step, you deploy your troops. Manipulate the selected participants subtly, get them to do your dirty work, let them draw their own conclusions. Manipulate reports, data, and communication. Sow doubts about the project's feasibility. Make use of the decision-makers' preferences and aversions.

Execute Execute the activities according to a plan. Getting a project disbanded does not take place by chance. Assess the effect of your actions and if necessary drop an additional bomb.

How to catch the project saboteur

As a project saboteur acts in the dark, it is not easy to find out whether you are actually under attack by one.

To find out if your project currently is being manipulated, you apply the Manipulation Facts Analysis. Although this analysis does not provide you with a black and white answer, it does give you an answer whether the project runs outside the normal project boundaries or not. The project saboteur always targets his manipulation at the means that the project manager uses to steer the project process. With the Manipulation Facts Analyses you investigate the actual course of the project and the daily events of the project in relation to the project process and result.

The matrix shows which irregularities might be occurring in your project.

If a low number of these irregularities occur in your project, you're lucky! But if more than 8 of these irregularities occur in your project, it is wise to renew your stakeholder analysis, and find out who might be the saboteur.

One final piece of advice: if you decide to counter attack your project saboteur, always consider your options compared with the options of the project saboteur. Choose your battles!

	Process	Result
Course	• Composition/mandate project board; the real decision makers are not on the project board. • Business case is missing. • Approval for the assignment is missing. • Approval for the planning is missing. • The project plan is incomplete. • Finance for the project is not covered by department budgets. • Responsibilities have not been defined. • Formal communication lines have not been established.	• Execution started with an undetermined scope. • Requirements for the project result are missing. • The design phase of the project started, although the requirements are incomplete or have not been approved. • Designs have not been approved. • The build phase of the project started, although the designs have not been approved. • The users have no requirements for the end result. • An extreme amount of changes. • Approval of milestones as well as results is missing.
Event	• The project board does not take and/or record decisions. • Discussions are continuously followed by new problems. • Most discussions concern the project process rather than the project result. • Necessary specialists are kept out of the project for more important projects. • Procedures are being used to block decision making. • Formal meeting schedules block the decision making process. • Reports show no issues or an extreme amount of issues (reporting outside the bandwidth). • Reported issues do not lead to solution measures. • Frequently replacing project members. • Corrective measures and or decisions are taken based on rumors rather than on formal reporting.	• An extreme amount of changes is being initiated • The scope is being changed continuously; new specialists have the opportunity to change the scope. • Project products are not being reviewed; specialist/users do not have the time to do so • Meetings about a solution, the requirements or other aspects always end with more questions than they started with. • Every proposed solution is proven unfeasible • The specialists present non-verifiable blockades.

Integrity and ethics

Prof dr. Muel Kaptein, from the Dutch Erasmus Research Institute of Management, is the author of a book titled, 'Why good people sometimes take wrong actions'.

He discovered the following split of actors: 1% is corrupt, 1% is incorruptible and 98% act according to the situation.

Members of the situational group are easy to influence and hence a good target for sabotage. If their own interest is properly serviced, they will act unethically and can manipulate or sabotage your project.

3 | Sabotaging the project's bureaucracy

You have done your project saboteur self-assessment and you have a good idea of the CRIME method. So far, so good. Now we take the next step: how do you undermine the bureaucracy of a project? If you want to understand fully how you can de-rail a project, you must understand the machinery that keeps a project in motion. That machinery is the bureaucracy. The operation of this bureaucracy and your relationship with the rules, roles and agreements determine which undermining methods you can best deploy as a project saboteur.

> *The word 'saboteur' dates from the industrial revolution when workers would throw their clogs (sabot in French) into the new looms to bring the machine to an immediate stop in the case of an emergency. The word sabotage took on its current meaning when the method was used to thwart the competition.*

The power of the bureaucrat is derived from management's pressing need to reduce uncertainty. The larger the company, the greater the need for a bureaucracy. The bureaucrats want to make a complex company transparent for management so they tell the manager whether or not any profit is being made, which departments spend too much money, draw up the annual budgets, and assess plans and reports. But a project requires courage and an entrepreneurial mindset and that doesn't fit comfortably into the operation of a bureaucracy, which has raised control to an ideology.

> "A lie gets halfway around the world before the truth has a chance to get its pants on."
>
> Sir Winston Churchill

As a project saboteur, you have to feed this bureaucratic monster. To do this, it helps to have a thorough knowledge of the organisation's regulations and to know the preferences and aversions of the bureaucrats. Your aim is to ensure that so much time is spent on tracking, supervising and adapting the rules that any progress and creativity in the project is blocked. In the following section you can read how you can approach this effectively and without causing any fuss.

The bureaucrats create the demand, the project manager supplies that demand. In this game of supply and demand, you must focus on the party creating the demand. The bureaucrats have insufficient knowledge about the project and this allows you, as a project saboteur, to supply them with information that is not found in any of the reports. This information reveals that the project is not under control (this does not, needless to say, need to be completely accurate information).

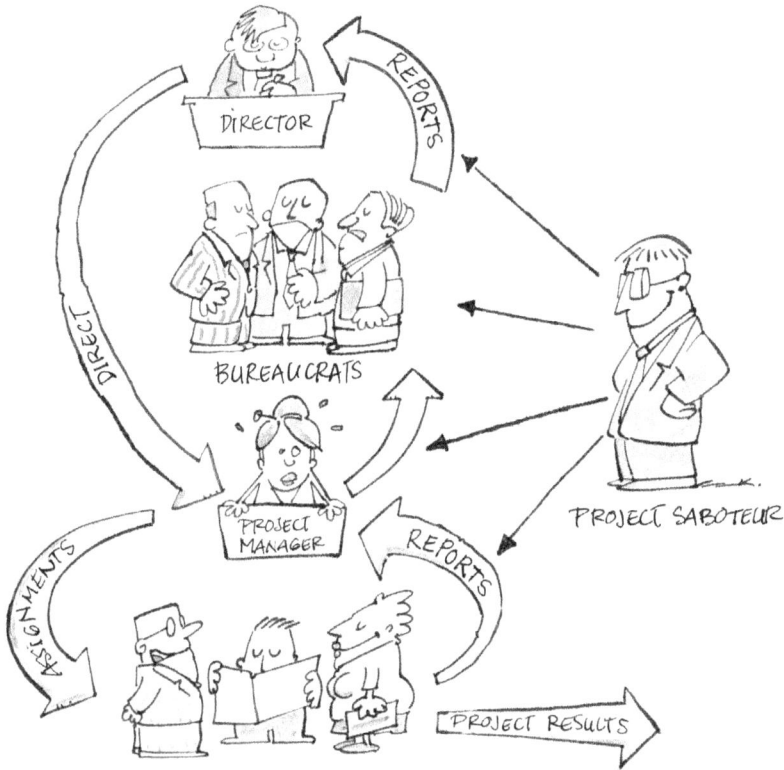

The content of the project report (the work of the project manager) appears to be incomplete or even inaccurate. The effect of this action is both miraculous and predictable: the bureaucrats demand additional information from the project manager; they tighten the bureaucratic thumb-screws. In the best case scenario, they will inform the director of their distrust. The director decides that reports must be made more frequently and must be far more detailed; and he stipulates that every change must be approved by him personally. Any last remains of creativity disappear from the project. The objective of the project manager is no longer to achieve a fine result, but to avoid being blamed for any mistakes. In other words, he starts to cover his ass.

You must also remember that for reporting one form is simply not enough. Each target group must receive its own specific report: one for management, one for the financial department and one for the international auditor. Make sure that the frequencies of these reports differ: the financial reports generally appear once a month, while the project progress reports must be made weekly. The fact that this creates a lot of additional work is a nice side effect; it doesn't make things move faster and can result in inconsistencies between the various reports. The project disappears into the top drawer in a way that is bureaucratically justified.

Bureaucracy demands a methodical approach. As a project saboteur, this gives you two alternate strategies:

The first is to *prevent* a *method* being adopted. After all, according to most literature, a method can have a beneficial effect on success.

The second is to aim for the *exaggeration of the method*: the project is set up in such a structured manner that there is absolutely no way of getting it moving. Furthermore, this gives the project saboteur an important tool: he is always fully aware of what the next stage of the project is and where he can find the next target for his subversive activities. Many people in and around the project desire a methodical approach. A good methodology gives certainty in something as uncertain as a project.

> *"Uncontrolled creativity without any discipline or process of innovation is at best distracting and at worst harmful to the organization,"*
>
> Paul Sloan in 'The Leader's Guide to Lateral Thinking Skills'

Read further about how you can undermine a project by being over-methodical or under-methodical.

Under methodical

Preventing the application of a methodology is fairly easy as many a project manager feels that a method means a lot of unnecessary work. He is required to fill in templates and has to do a lot of writing which he doesn't feel like doing at all. In addition, a method requires him to provide a lot of useless information that he believes makes little contribution to the end result. Without a method, his experience means that he already works in an extremely structured and effective way. The course he has to follow about the method used in the company contains little news: he's been using it for years, even if it's been given a different name. The project manager's conclusion is that there is little extra value in following the methodology; all it means is extra paper-work. This provides the project saboteur with an ideal basis for sowing doubt about following the method and the risk this could entail.

A second target is the director. You can make him believe that following the methodology is no guarantee for a successful result. The project manager will simply fill in templates. If the result is disappointing, the project manager will have indicated this in a structured way. After all, he's doing the reporting isn't he? Of course he forgot to implement measures, but the director and the steering group had all the necessary information and knew what was going on.

Most directors have experience with project managers who use a project management methodology to cover their asses. Emphasise to the director that a more direct way of reporting — for example, verbally — is much more efficient and effective. Methodologies and reports offer false security. Stress the director's experience: he has undertaken projects in the past, he is an experienced expert. It doesn't take much effort to get him to admit that he knows what takes place in projects, that he will feel when something is not quite right in a project. "I don't need reports for that", you hear him say.

If you want to undermine a project, it's a good idea to throw some cogs in the bureaucratic wheels.

Over methodical

> "Concepts which have proved useful for ordering things easily
> assume so great an authority over us, that we forget their terrestrial
> origin and accept them as unalterable facts. They then become
> labelled as `conceptual necessities', etc. The road of scientific
> progress is frequently blocked for long periods by such errors. It is
> therefore not just an idle game to exercise our ability to analyze
> familiar concepts, and to demonstrate the conditions on which this
> justification of their usefulness depends."
>
> Albert Einstein

Exaggerating a method also gives the saboteur a good chance of success. After all, who doesn't want to make sure that the project can be managed and verified? Project management methodologies are, without exception, aimed at the manageability and verification of the project. Modern organisations go so far as to stipulate which project management method and reporting standards must be used.

There are regulations for requesting additional budget, for recording decisions and for setting up project files. These organisations force projects into a bureaucratic corset and restrict the creativity necessary to achieve a good project result. The bureaucrats in the organisation have considerable influence; they provide the management with information that forms the basis for important decisions. They indicate whether or not the project is on schedule, and at the same time force the project manager to adhere to the reporting standards.

Bureaucrats have an unhealthy fixation on generating reports; they have turned the means into the end. It is more lethal for a project manager to forget a report than to produce a bad result. And so the bureaucrats become the involuntary accomplices of the project saboteur.

As a project saboteur, you encourage the application of the method to the extreme. Every project stage must be properly completed before the following can begin. First, insist on an approved plan, and only then, its implementation. A methodical approach also requires that the employees keep a meticulous record of the time they spend on the project Any suspicion you may have that there is the slightest deviation from the method should be immediately reported to your bureaucrat friends. They will then warn the director for you about the approaching doom and apply the brakes to the project.

The players

It should by now be clear that you have many weapons at your disposal as a project saboteur. But it is less self-evident which of these weapons you should or should not deploy. That depends on your position in the organisation, on your knowledge and on your relationships.

If you are a manager in the organisation you can make use of your formal powers. As specialist, you can make use of your knowledge to disrupt a project. If you are an employee in a change project, then you are at the source of all-that-is-evil and can directly influence the results. If you are an end-user of the result, the project requires your knowledge of the current work process, which in turn gives you other possibilities for sending the project off in the wrong direction.

To give you a better idea of your possibilities, we will take a closer look at the following players:

- the Director;
- the Project Manager;
- the User;
- the Specialist;
- the member of the Joint Consultative Committee (JCC).

In the following chapters we will highlight a number of undermining possibilities for each of these players, and show you how to apply them in practice.

You should, of course, read about your own role! But don't forget to read about the other roles. Only then will you see how others can influence your project. Furthermore, it will allow you to decide who you can and want to involve in your plot. You can read how to do this effectively in the chapter 'Conspiracy'.

How to counter attack the project saboteur

One aspect to mention here: acknowledge the fact that sabotage simply exists. That applies to all players, by the way. The world does not consist of 100% reliable and trustworthy people. Some have a huge personal interest that makes them act contrary to the interest of the project, rather than acting according to the general interest. There are not many projects that do not suffer from sabotage activities.

The first question to be answered is how important is the project saboteur to the project. If the knowledge or organisational influence of the saboteur is crucial for your project, in that case you have to try to convert your opponent into a supporter of the project. With the stakeholder analysis you already determined why the saboteur wants to manipulate your project. Per reason you determined, define and implement a counter measure that solves his resistance against the project. This sounds rather easy and in many cases it is. For example, if the project result is a threat for the position of the saboteur offer him an alternative position.

If you are not depending on the saboteur, then the counter attack is obvious: break all connections of this project saboteur with the project. This sounds simple but in many cases it is not. Many of these saboteurs have a large informal network they use to influence the management of the organisation.

Sometimes you are not in the position to implement the counter measures yourself; in that case you have to involve the right decision maker.

But be aware: this decision maker might be the real saboteur!

Project success

The Standish Group lists 10 factors of success and relates them to the factors that increase value. The result is a more complete view on what makes the world go round. It also shows that success is not entirely the same as creating a value- based approach: 60% of the factors overlap.

The Factors of Success are: (the relevance is expressed in points per factor)

The Factors of Success are: (the relevance is expressed in points per factor)		The Factors of Value are: (the relevance is again expressed in points per factor)	
Executive Sponsorship	15	Small Projects	35
Emotional Maturity	15	Optimizing Business Value	20
User Involvement	15	More Risks and Failures	10
Optimisation	15	Executive Sponsorship	8
Skilled Resources	10	Emotional Maturity	7
SAME*	8	Agile Process	6
Agile Process	7	Tuned in	5
Modest Execution	6	Lean Execution	4
Project Management Expertise	5	Talented Staff	3
Clear Business Objectives	4	SAME*	2

Standard Architectural Management Environment, a group of integrated practices and services.

Source: Standish Group, Factors of Value, 2015

The conclusion is that in the factors of success and in the factors of value, the human factor is not highly dominant. Even 'Emotional Stability' and 'User Involvement' are not about the self-interest of people. And that interest is what we consider to be a major factor in turning project failure into project success!

4 | The undermining director

As the director, you stand at the head of the project empire; you make the decisions for each stage of the project. Project control is your instrument for bringing about the failure of the project.

You have the final say in which project manager is appointed. You issue the project assignment and the project manager draws up the plan that you approve or reject. It can be in the interests of the director for the project to be a failure. He could perhaps consider the project very threatening for his own department, but would prefer to have the project fail rather than to oppose it from the start. *Designed to fail* is what we call this. He may issue the order for its execution, but can perhaps do nothing else in his position because he has in turn been given the order by, for example, the Supervisory Board.

Select the right project manager

As undermining director, you manipulate the selection of the project manager. Your aim is to appoint a project manager who is not capable and who can be influenced. For this, you have the choice between three kinds of candidates with the wrong sorts of motivation: somebody who sees it as a step in his career, somebody who doesn't mind doing a project on the side or a project manager with little experience.

The first kind is *the candidate who sees it as a step in his career.* He is less interested in the project than in his own position. Often, such a candidate has little or no experience in leading a project and will quickly be inclined to seek assistance — an ideal candidate! As director, you naturally have a suitable person in mind when he requests an assistant. You have somebody standing by who will carry out your orders much better than those from the project manager. In this way, you have a spy in place who can report on the true status of the project.

In comparison, *the manager who does it on the side* is quickly inclined to assume full responsibility; little stimulus is needed for this. This type of manager always bites off more than he can chew; he's an easy target. You make grateful use of this characteristic and load him up with an enormous amount of work. You can easily off-load an extra project onto this project scourge; he always overestimates his abilities. An excellent way of wrong footing this jack-of-all-trades is to demand immediate answers to a whole lot of urgent problems. Increase his scope, ask him questions about the yield of the project, even if that isn't part of his job. There is, after all, nobody else in the organisation who possesses the necessary qualities to solve this problem. It is highly unlikely that this project manager will admit that it's all too much for him, but gradually things will start to unravel.

Finally, there is the *inexperienced project manager*: he too will be eager to assist, and you are only too pleased to grant him his request. If you do not have a suitable candidate who can act as an experienced assistant, then you will have to hire in somebody from outside. This can be risky; there are some highly qualified candidates out there. The wrong candidates are dyed-in-the-wool experts in the field of project management. You can easily keep these at bay; you are, after all, looking for an *assistant*. Assistant and administration are fortunately terms that are closely associated with each other. You strongly urge engaging a young project administrator (low fees, no project experience). The inexperienced project manager will look for certainty and somebody to hold on to; a stability you can offer him as director. You stimulate his weaknesses; and if he nevertheless starts showing signs of professional behaviour, you reward him by demanding a different report, by changing the assignment, by removing specialists from the project, and above all by taking no decisions. When the project manager thinks he has his report down to a tee, you ask him about something totally different. Present him with problems that he did not begin to know existed. Ask him, for example, after some time has passed whether his solution is SOX compliant. The project manager will go pale; he doesn't dare to admit that he doesn't know what you're talking about. Panic in the project. The focus is suddenly shifted to assessing the SOX problem and is no longer on delivering the project result.

Withhold the project assignment

The project assignment is given to the project manager at the start of the project. As director, it's your job to approve the assignment. This is where you have maximum influence. The first tactic is *to delay approval*. Or rather: don't give any approval; your aim is to prevent the legitimacy of the project assignment. If there is still no assignment, you have set the basis for extremely fuzzy project control. In whose name does the project manager speak? Is he actually authorised to do what he's doing? This will prove paralysing.

The project manager knows that the company needs the project results; greater efficiency can be achieved. So what does the courageous project manager do? He makes a start. He engages (external) staff in the expectation that approval is forthcoming, and sets off on his adventure. This worthy project manager allows himself to be led like a lamb to the slaughter! The project assignment hasn't been granted, so as the director it's easy to put the project manager on the back foot. "Why do you think we implemented a method for project development in the company? So that we follow all the right steps! And what happens here? No assignment, but you've started anyway! You can't run a business like that. If everybody decided to start projects without formal approval, we'd be in a sorry mess! And what exactly do you think the task of management is? Approving things after they've been done?" With this attitude — perfectly correct in itself — you can, as undermining director, win a further delay of several weeks.

It is not difficult to allow the project manager to get started without permission. Most project managers know that it can prove extremely tricky to get final approval! A director doesn't really want to accept the responsibility for a project: just imagine if things went wrong. By allowing a project to get under way without formal approval, you create a very good reason for having to stop it at a later date. The ideal situation is when the project manager is still young, willing and ambitious. He wants to get on with his project and not wait around until all the formalities are completed; that would be a waste of valuable time.

A second delaying tactic is to keep the assignment as vague as possible. Leave the scope unclear, describe in ambiguous terms what must be achieved when the project is completed. That gives you the possibility of putting your foot on the brake once the project has gained momentum. In many cases, a vague project assignment is better than no assignment at all; the project manager has the impression that he is acting legitimately. Some project managers prefer a vague assignment to a more concrete one; it allows them to decide the content of the project in the way they see fit. As undermining director, you can handily interpret the assignment by making clear to the project manager at predetermined times that he is not delivering what has been agreed. As director, you are always in the right; after all, you are the person who granted the assignment, and if the project manager didn't understand what you intended then the least you could have expected from a well-paid professional is that he should ask you what you meant. Always aim for an unclear, incomplete assignment that is open to a multitude of interpretations. Such an assignment will prove a source for manipulation.

Manipulate planning and reports

The foundation of a successful project is a good plan, which indicates in detail what must happen when, in which order and for which costs. The project manager draws up such a plan at the start of the project and uses this as a reference for his reports. As undermining director, you must prevent a good plan. Without such a reference, reports will be unreliable.

In addition, you have, as the undermining director, influence on the budgets. You have two parameters here: the amount of the budget and its availability. Most project managers expect that the director will do his utmost to make any budget shortfall available. After all, it is in the director's interest that the project succeeds. If there is an insufficient budget at the start of the project, he will not consider this an insurmountable problem. That gives the undermining director a nice advantage.

Another remarkable phenomenon arises in reporting. Imagine: the project has just got under way, it has started with a clean slate. The reports about the budgets give reassuringly low figures, for example, 3% of the staff budget has been used up. And what is 3%? Still 97% to go! It is a rule of thumb that at the start, the prognosis is always equal to the budgeted amounts. That is hardly remarkable: an estimate has only just be made (when the project was drawn up), and a subsequent estimate made just shortly afterwards is not likely to show any deviation.

But that 3% may have been spent in the completely wrong way. As the undermining director, however, you allow yourself to be reassured. As the project progresses, the picture changes: the percentage of the resources used increase, and the chance that a *deviation* is projected also increases. As director you can make grateful use of this. You do not accept any deviation whatsoever. How? Simple: from the very start you make it perfectly clear to the project manager that the project results must be delivered for the agreed amount, within the agreed time. Since the project manager has made a careful prognosis concerning how much of the budget will be used, you hold him to it. Strictly. There is, however, one thing that you manipulate: the scope. Because you did not agree everything clearly in advance, you request, within the bounds of the vagueness of the assignment, additional functionality, more than was budgeted for.

And every time the project manager splutters in disapproval, you remind him of the agreement that he would deliver on time within the stipulated budget. The inexperienced project manager will now return to his team and put them under pressure. The demands the project manager will make of his team are almost inhuman. When the first casualties to sickness occur, the project comes to a creaking standstill.

In the exceptional case that the team still manages to make progress, you then adopt a different plan: you decide, in the interests of the organisation, to have the project audited. It goes without saying that this audit must be paid from the project budget, adding a little extra pressure to the project. The nice thing about a project under pressure is that the project members reduce all sorts of unimportant matters — such as documentation, assessment of the results and testing — to the minimum. The audit flawlessly brings these problems to light. Not only does the audit cost the project members a great deal of time, the repair work will result in further delay.

The availability of project members also gives you, the undermining director, considerable influence. The project manager needs specialists from the organisation. You assure him verbally that you will take care of it. But the specialists you allocate are indispensable for the day-to-day operation of the business. The department manager is not prepared to sacrifice his staff to the project when they are required; daily production is, after all, more important than the project. The conflicting priorities between the line organisation and the project always lead to delay. You must therefore stimulate such conflicts. When the time arrives to deploy specialists, you choose the side of the department manager.

Planning and reporting are essential components of project management for you as the director; they are instruments for effectively disrupting the project.

There is no direct reporting about the progress of the project to you, the director: the project manager is your buffer. On the one hand this is logical because he must select the team reports, interpret them and present them as a concise whole. This places the project manager in an ideal position to conceal the truth and present things in a different light. You must assume that he will do this, particularly when he is put under increasing pressure. The project manager will report that the project can continue because it seems to be progressing well. But you know better: distrust all reports!

There is a similar buffer between the project manager and the project team. You should ensure that you have a scout, somebody who can feed you information. A good tactic is proposing somebody who doesn't really want the change either, but is very well informed about the content. When you drop in on the project, that person is the one you talk to; you'll find he'll tell you everything that's going wrong with the project and what people are trying to hide. You will even learn what the project team is concealing from the project manager.

I HOPE WE CAN MAKE UP
FOR LOST TIME

THEY'RE WORKING HARD AND
WE ARE RIGHT ON SCHEDULE

In most cases, you, as the director of a project, also have a boss. This boss, often a member of the management team or of the supervisory board, is the person who appointed you. You are acting as a director on his behalf. Your boss, obviously, has more authority than you do, and there is always the possibility of him intervening. If you are to give your boss the chance of intervening, you must ensure that he doesn't interfere at the start of the project and you must on no account inform him about progress. There is no better reason for the executive board or the supervisory board to stop the project than not knowing anything about it. They have the authority and power to halt the project. If they are left in the dark, they will develop a high level of distrust about the progress of the project. Add to this the perfectly natural inclination for the person who has been ignored to want to take revenge on the person who ignored him — and sabotage becomes a reality.

The directors as saboteurs

Where the directors step-by-step engineer the downfall of the project, while openly supporting it.

An international insurance company is made up of a potpourri of units that, until recently, had all been independent. The company has grown by constantly acquiring other insurance companies. And all these companies have their own processes and computer systems. When the next major acquisition takes place, all the talk — it is business as usual — is about more synergy, building up service centres instead of cost centres, and achieving efficiency and cost reduction by concentrating activities.

All this talk must be turned into action. A major project for streamlining all processes and computerisation is set up.

From the very start it is all too clear that the individual business units do not support the idea at all. They are large, profitable and have worked independently for years. But they are also well aware of the wishes of the Executive Board: reduce costs by co-operating more. Open disagreement with this wish, which is also laid down in strategic business plans, is clearly not an option. It is remarkable to see that the management of all the units involved (the units each boast several thousand employees) choose a subversive tactic. Officially they support the strategic plans, but in practice they delay the project.

One of the strategic plans involves setting up a service centre for a number of activities including banking services. This service centre falls under the company's top management; it is, after all, an umbrella activity for the whole company. The executive board realises that a strong hand is needed to get the centre off the ground and appoints a very ambitious project director. He reports to the central board and thus has a certain say over the business units concerned.

Ideal conditions are now created for generating resistance: the business units realise that the plans will erode their independence and their size; the overambitious project director draws up an ambitious plan and starts whipping everybody into action; centralised and decentralised responsibilities are at odds with each other; and the vision of the future is not shared by everybody.

The project director foresees a number of problems and invites the directors of the business units to form the steering committee of the project organisation. In this way, or so he thinks, they will not be able to circumnavigate the decision-making process. There is now an official group of directors. Clearly, they have mixed feelings about the whole thing. But, as already mentioned, refusal is not an option; after all, the Board of Management has given the plan its wholehearted support.

Very quickly, the strategic plans are translated to the operational level. The project organisation makes an inventory of the units, which are governed by the project. To leverage the maximum cost reduction, as many people as possible will have to be transferred to the new service centre. It was predictable that the business units have completely different ideas about that. They start their disguised resistance. To begin with, their definition of the services that will fall under the service centre is totally different to those drawn up by the project organisation. A lot, naturally, is decentralised, and all those decentralised processes are, of course, so unique that they cannot be lumped together.

There are, needless to say, departments perfectly suited for this, and these are listed by the management of the business units. These departments, however, do not share this vision. They may have been officially nominated, but the advantages of merging escapes them. What's more, these departments are spread throughout the country; they are concerned that centralisation of these business units will mean they will have to relocate. Since the departments are in the south, north and east of the country and the central units in the west, this will mean that it will be more expensive and a lot busier for those having to relocate. They are not inclined to cooperate in their own demise. Through the grapevine, people are well aware that the department managers say they support the plans, but that they have considerable reservations about things. That means that the employees feel they will enjoy support if they do not respond quickly to questions from the project organisation.

A long drawn-out process emerges. The project director sees that he is making little progress. He has requested and received official support from the Board of Management for the project, but that doesn't seem to be working. Now he ponders his next move. That is about control. If the business units refuse to hand over their activities, let us at least place the financial responsibility for those units under the new service centre. He who pays the piper, is his reasoning. The Board of Management approves this step and within a few months the financial responsibility for the activities to be relocated is placed in the hands of the director of the service centre in development — in this case, the ambitious project director. Strictly speaking, he now has a stranglehold on the situation.

The management of the business units, however, is not planning to give up gracefully. They watch on as the change in financing takes place, but they have an alternative. Officially there is no choice; practice proves otherwise. They finance their activities from other resources that are still controlled by their own budgets. The actual authority over the activities remains in the hand of the managements and the project director loses an important instrument of control. The project director is still unable to make sufficient progress.

The progress is monitored in the steering committee meetings. People see that a lot of activity is taking place, but also that results are lacking. Why aren't the processes not yet known? The project director indicates that the people required for this are insufficiently available. He gets in more staff from outside in order to keep on schedule.

After six months, questions arise about the progress of the project. Why hasn't the planning been met? The discussion is not about the existing organisation, but about the project. There are increasing doubts about the capabilities of the project director. It also becomes clear that the project has gone enormously over budget. The steering committee grumbles. Finally they get what they want: an investigation is set up. The investigation has to meet two conditions: the project must be put on hold and the investigation must be undertaken by an external party. During the investigation, momentum is lost, and so too are many crucial staff (including those hired in).

The next stage is a foregone conclusion: the project dies.

The business units can breathe easily again; their staff can remain where they are, their own self-interests have been served.

The result for the company is: no synergy, no savings, but an additional expense for the project of around £22 million.

Tips for the sabotaging project director:

- Make sure there is a project manager who is not capable

- Prevent a legitimate, authorised assignment for the project

- Make the assignment and its scope vague. The higher the level of abstraction, the easier it is to obtain agreement

- Make sure the plan lacks any sort of cohesion

- Prevent cooperation and resources being made available, and certainly if they are essential

- Have things get under way without parameters such as a good network planning?

- Start before all employees are present

- Adhere strictly to budget and timing

- Increase the pressure on the project to an inhuman level

- Implement changes within the vague scope

- Stimulate conflicting priorities between project and line organisation

- Recruit partners in crime, infiltrators in the project

- Do not provide management with any information

Investigate the director's actions

The first step to see if you have a director with a sabotage risk is to refer to the questionnaire in Chapter 1 and execute the project manipulation stakeholder analysis. With this list you check the motives, the mentality, the influence and the knowledge of the director. If the outcome of your investigation is that it could be in the interest of the director to manipulate the project, watch it!

The next step is to look at the facts: execute the Manipulation Facts Analyses as described in chapter 2. If a high number of irregularities caused by the director occur, have a closer look.

The director is crucial in the starting and planning phases of a project. Carefully watch his planning and finance activities. Watch out for 'plan till you drop', a regular sabotage and delay trick. It is simply impossible to plan the future. The main purpose of a plan is to define to what extent reality differs from your plan. Better to apply Henry Mintzbergs' emergent strategies. That is, to plan only short term and adjust your plan frequently as you go. But do keep the long-term goal in mind. Where finance is concerned: is the required budget well estimated?

If both steps convince you that indeed there is a risk connected with the director as a person and indeed his actions can only be explained if sabotage is at play, then have a look at the measures.

The first and foremost measure in order to have a successful director is to align his interests with that of the project. Any deviation from that starting point will persuade him not to follow the project's goal. If, for instance, his project leads to a serious staff reduction of his own department, he will not make the required project speed. If, on the other hand, he will be promoted, if successful, that is a different ball game. Simple? Yes! Often applied? No!

The director might hide behind the conflict of interest between the project organization and the regular line organization. A common trick in the book. Promote just one common interest: that of the company as a whole. Any deviation from that principle is devastating.

So, if you think the director is a sabotage risk and he is demonstrating suspicious progress facts, it is time to take measures. It's better to replace him at an early stage than give him the opportunity to slow down or even destroy the project.

Keep in mind that for replacing the director you must be in a suitable position with the correct, powerful mandate. As a project manager, for instance, you might need an independent third party to assist, like the internal audit department or the external auditor.

How adequate is the reporting in three UK departments?

The reports we see do not always reveal the actual reasons of project delays. A few examples:

- The UK Home Office runs a project called 'Transferring the Customer Experience'. The Major Project Authority reviewed the project and gave it a red status.
  The Home Office was asked to report on the lack of progress and responded as follows:
  "The programme is making progress and is in the latter stages of application software delivery".

And:

"At the reporting point the programme was working on a re-phased plan to accommodate operational capacity and now forecasts a revised end date of 01/11/2014."

- The Ministry of Defence also experienced a red UK Major Project Authority status on their Defence Information Infra-structure (DII) project. And what the report said:
"DII is taking (......) action to bring the remaining delivery challenges into line under a robust risk-adjusted plan".

- The Ministry of Justice in the UK runs a project on Shared Services. The Project "will deliver a transformation in the approach to the provision of back office services in MoJ".
A red alert was granted by the UK Cabinet Office, the Major Project Authority, to this project. The Ministry of Justice reported as follows:
"The programme has completed a restructure and has made new appointments to the leadership team to ensure that individuals with relevant experience and skills are in place to drive the current stage of the programme."

Source: UK Cabinet Office, Major Project Authority, 2013 Annual Report.

Three examples of superficial reporting. Are they covering up the truth? Are the real reasons for the red alert mentioned? Is there some manipulation on the facts going on? What was the reason why the right staff was not available?

5 | The sabotaging project manager

As project manager, you play a key role in the project; you direct the day-to-day business and this puts you in an excellent position to destroy the project.

As project manager, your power is considerable: you are the fulcrum in the balance of power between client and steering group. You know the project inside out and decide what should be reported and what should be kept under wraps. And the steering group? We all know that it's called that because you steer clear of it. They aren't the ones who do the steering? No, of course not. They are steered by you, the undermining project manager.

As project manager, you steer your team and you decide what information gets passed on and what is held back. You have influence on every choice in the project. You can conscript employees into your teams and you can fire them. It is you who determines the success or failure of the project. In this chapter you can read about what you can do to ensure the demise of the project.

Select your director?

You always have one client. As sabotaging project manager, you would do well to determine whether there is more than one candidate who could claim the role of client. It is extremely rare if this is not the case. For example, the assignment is inter-departmental, involving several business units. In such a case, one clear vision from one department is not desirable. You are in a perfect position to stimulate the competence struggle between the various people responsible. You do this by giving people the feeling that they have been ignored. Tell the departments yourself about the project and the consequences it will have for them. The nice thing is that this is actually part of your job as project manager. They will sound the alarm. Of course, you can also inform one of the forgotten groups after the project is under way. The non-involved departments will want to be involved and will do everything possible to have the project suspended. The human psyche comes to your help here: when a manager is ignored, this does little good for his prestige. He will then be inclined to do everything in his power to have the project disbanded. The reason for sounding the alarm is not that the project is getting out of hand – no: the power of a manager is under siege. The world will have to understand that he is not to be ignored. Maslow lesson one (see appendix B).

Manipulate your project assignment

As sabotaging project manager, you must make sure that you give yourself as much room as possible for sabotaging the project. It's not all that difficult to carry out a vague assignment, in fact, most clients do not know exactly what they want and are extremely happy if you, a competent project manager, are nevertheless prepared to go ahead with it. This gives you the all the room you need for effectively sabotaging the project. The characteristics of a vague assignment are intangible terms such as 'usable' and 'suitable for the purpose'. You must avoid a verifiable aim. In addition, it is handy if the customer of the result is unknown; after all, if you are doing things for somebody you don't know, you have a chance of engaging extremely critical reviewers and approvers on the way. What's more, you give yourself the opportunity of attracting a greater number of interested parties.

If your client turns out to be one of those annoying types – you know, one who thinks he knows what he wants – you should help him define a very rigid assignment with an incredibly detailed list of requirements, which leaves no room whatsoever for flexibility. The more requirements the better, for that increases the chance of contradictory demands. It is highly unlikely that the specialists will know the requirements, let alone that they take them all into account in the solution. This will provide a perfect reason for having to reject the result.

Keep your project plan vague

Your project plan describes the scenario that you will use as project manager to achieve the project result. If you are to have little chance of success, it is essential that your plan is weak on content. But in the eyes of your client, this plan must provide a solid basis for the project.

To achieve that, the plan has to look perfect (and that is not difficult with modern Desk Top publishing techniques). Include a few simple graphically well-designed charts,. An image is appealing and, if it is to be understood, should contain few details. It is then made 'at management level'. Tell the decision-makers that you have only included the main lines; you don't want to bother them with details. Flatter their ego by referring to overcrowded schedules; the details are for the project members.

A few important tips for an unsound plan:

- Keep the scope and aim of the project vague. Projects without an aim can be easily torpedoed.

- Only describe the hierarchy, the structure of the project, in extremely general terms. Only appoint the main players. All this can fuel discussions about competence (and ego), which block progress and feed the distrust between the parties.

- Do not plan all stages, just the first; the rest will follow.

- Do not designate a time estimate to all tasks. Mention a few, so that you create the appearance of accuracy. You will have thus laid the foundation for the project running over time.

- Specify the resources and the budgets for part of the duration of the project.

- Restrict the personnel planning; do not name all participants in the project. Do not concern yourself with details: familiarisation time, deployability and productivity percentages. Do not describe any criteria they must satisfy. Experience shows that the client will not ask you about the selection criteria you have used for the personnel.

- Do not show who will communicate with whom, when and about what; do not make a communications plan. Communications in the project must grow organically: we will identify communication needs as and when they arise during the project, and we will adapt things accordingly. Your argument is flexibility. You are basing your theory on a pseudo management bestseller: 'Theory of the Loosely-Coupled Organic Networks'. Let's see if anybody dares to admit not having this bestseller on his bookshelf!

• Nobody will miss the documentation plan if you do not include it. But the effect it can have is remarkable! Documents get lost, directives are not followed, design decisions are not recorded. End result? Work is done on the wrong versions: a source of pleasure when you want to disrupt the project.

Use the people in your environment

As undermining project manager you do not just have to deal with employees, but also with future users and other interested parties in the environment of the project. You may not, of course, direct them all yourself, but they are all dependent on your information.

Your project team

Claim complete freedom in conscripting your project members. The details of this task should not concern your client. It goes without saying that you select people who fit with your sabotage strategy. Roughly speaking, your project team is made up of administrators and specialists. For the first group, find really high quality people. For example, somebody who knows programs like PowerPoint, Excel and Project inside out and can use them to give your communications a necessary touch of slickness. For the specialists, things are somewhat different: they are chosen because they understand their profession and so you should somewhat restrict the quality of these members. You do this by choosing inexperienced specialists and by putting together an unbalanced team of specialists. Select specialists who are disciples of different schools of methodology. You could, for example, have an architect specialised in *component-based development* cooperate with somebody who finds the classical *data-oriented approach* more attractive. You can bet that they will spend more time discussing the approach rather than the solution. Another useful player is the person who designed the solution that is now up for replacement. He is a potential sabotaging ally; after all, the project is intending to murder his brainchild.

Your project suppliers

Some of your resources are the employees of the suppliers of the project. You have no direct say over the matter, but you can influence the choice. Use your network; you remember somebody. In this way, you create a liaison man or woman in your environment with a crucial supplier. If a supplier threatens to add a highly qualified specialist to his team, use your informal channels to suggest that you are dubious about the qualities of that specialist. Most suppliers will generally refrain from pushing forward the employee. Another approach is to encourage the specialist to minimise his contribution to the project. Make sure that it comes to his attention (indirectly) that you question his abilities. This generally results in resistance, ensuring your prophecy comes true. Consciously or otherwise, he is not going to waste his time on your project.

Your users

The users are an interesting group for you and, as an undermining project manager, they can be readily manipulated. They are involved in drawing up the requirements and accepting the result. Make sure the user does not have sufficient authority. His advice and opinions are, of course, entirely valid, but if the rank and file do not support them, they can be easily dismissed. It is human nature that the user wishes to represent his department. He has, after all, been invited to participate because of his knowledge of the matter and that is flattering. He will quite likely be prepared to exceed his authority in order to be taken seriously by the project group. Stimulate him in this and do not let him consult too often with his rank and file. Once a considerable list of requirements has been drawn up, submit it to his rank and file: "Have you seen what's coming your way?" You've laid the groundwork for an almighty row: "Who agreed to all this and who does he think he's representing?"

Regularly replace the users during the course of the project. Having the same user throughout, somebody who thus knows the history of the project, greatly increases the chance of success. When the person involved in the acceptance test is somebody other than the person who drew up the requirements, he will probably reject the result. An argument to justify such a change is that the user should not lose his feeling with practical matters, a good reason for returning him to his department after several months. Career is another mechanism for replacing users. On the whole, normal work is better for a career than project work, because project work has a lower profile and is therefore less valued.

Objectivity is yet another argument: it is proper that somebody else should look at things after an appropriate amount of time has passed.

A practical issue is paying for the users' contribution. Generally, the deployment of a user has to be paid for. If you control that, you can steer the user's deployment. You should therefore make sure that the organisation supplying the user also pays for his deployment. The argument you use for this is that the user will also profit (in the long run) from the deployment. But if the project starts running over time, the department is likely to demand the return of its member; they've spent enough money already. And the discontinuity of important user knowledge arises all by itself.

The Bottom Rung of the Ladder

A very effective source of information – but one which is all too often underestimated – is the network of personal assistants, interns, and secretaries. A good relationship with your client's PA is a blessing. He can prove a fantastic source of information, either over a cup of coffee or during lunch. There is bound to be some information hidden away in all that small talk. You could, for example, learn that your client has a meeting next week with one of the suppliers and you immediately know who you must manipulate. Get in touch with the PA yourself; phone him, drop in and show understanding when something goes wrong. Your objective: information. Your tools: trust, understanding, respect and a sympathetic ear.

Misuse the project method

As mentioned earlier, project management methods are popular because they offer certainty. The methods are imposed and monitored by the bureaucrats, who have made it their life's ambition to make things as difficult as possible for you, the project manager. The cycle of plan, report and adjust is at the core of every project management method. If something goes wrong with the project, you, the project manager, will be able to defend yourself. You have, after all, reported at an early stage that something was threatening to go wrong. You promptly reported a deviation from the plan. That you didn't undertake any actions to rectify the situation is neither here nor there.

Reporting

Some project management methods stipulate the writing of an exception report: a fixed template in which you report a problem. You make an exception report, according to the standard, and submit it. Strangely enough, there is a good chance that that will be sufficient. The steering group that receives the report will see that there is a problem (that the project will over-run, for example), but will also see that this has been reported and that it will be under control. The key questions – "What have you done to solve it? and What was the result?" – are not asked. The bureaucrats are satisfied: you have submitted the report on time in complete compliance with the standard. What the bureaucrats fail to understand is that they are your Partners in Crime; they are the communication channel for all your false messages to management, which management blindly trusts.

As project manager, you do not want your director, the one who authorises the project, to have every detail. He can restrict your ability to steer things yourself. Be selective in your reporting. The advantage of that is that the client then can only steer selectively. He is not capable of reacting to matters that do not reach him.

In the meantime, you work on the destruction of the project. If you want the project to be stopped from one moment to the next, you choose the appropriate moment to leak the bad news. You have been carefully saving up all the various glitches and drawbacks and for you that means one thing: you've earned interest on them. They have grown into a mountain of misery. You create a shock effect and in this way bring the project to a sudden, shuddering halt. If you are applying the tactic of sparing the rod and spoiling the child and you want the project to become an increasingly malevolent delinquent, you should report the misery step by step, always in what would seem to be manageable bits.

The medium is the message

Something you should never forget is the packaging of the message: a report can be perfect in content and also be delivered on time, but if it looks unkempt, nobody will take it seriously. The opposite is also true: a mediocre content in a beautiful packaging increases the level of acceptance. Package your message well and make sure the report looks good. That increases trust. It can be attractively illustrated with surveys and graphs that standard reports demand. Often, something has been developed to show at a glance whether everything in the project is going according to plan. It could be a traffic light or a smiley. It doesn't take much effort to turn all the smilies 'green'. The result is that the administrators live under the supposition that things are reasonably under control. The reality will emerge in a process, which you, as sabotaging project manager, will carefully orchestrate.

An ancillary way of directing attention away from the content of the project is a flashy site on the intranet, where the project is described in easy terms. Frequently report successes. Send the link to all and sundry. The site is a source for manipulation. If you post information on the site that contradicts what is in the informal channels, then this will cause unrest. In many cases, such unrest leads to the client taking action, something that you can direct very efficiently. After all, you are feeding both the formal and the informal communication channels.

Make sure there's no money

Money is the most effective resource that you have available as sabotaging project manager. Money makes the project possible and is the generally accepted project facilitator. If there's no money, the project doesn't go ahead.

The client will soon pose the question: What will the result mean for the company? Will the benefits outweigh the costs? If the client has the impression that the company will not be better off, he will generally pull the plug on the project. More than enough reason to pause and ask how, as the sabotaging project manager, you can disrupt the project by concentrating on the money: the cost estimations, the budgets and the business case.

It is self-evident that a cost estimate will be drawn up at the start of a project. As project leader, you play a crucial role in this. You could simply think: make a very high estimate and the project will never be started. But that is far too easy. Take a look at the following ways of obstructing the cost estimate.

Short-term success through over-budgeting

Let's start with short-term success: if you are to be successful in the *short term*, you must make the cost estimate far too *high*. This will make it much more difficult to find the money required; high amounts always scare people off.

It is easier to have estimates set too high. Nothing is easier than saying, "in practice, things always turn out badly". Most people take that to heart; they are bothered about spending too much and want to showcase themselves as the guardians of the company's reserves. And practice shows: things really do always turn out badly.

> *"Budgeting: a method of being concerned before the money is spent instead of afterwards."*
>
> Voltaire

As project manager, you can always, at the start of a project, refer to published examples of projects that have run over budget, or better still, to a project within your own company.

An extremely detailed break-down of the project activities and their expected costs is particularly helpful. There is a very simple principle here: the more elements the break-down contains, the higher the total costs become. This is a psychological matter: one thing costs something, two things cost more.

Include the overhead costs: when you undertake a project, you generally make use of the existing infrastructure: office space, PCs, licences for software etc. Do not think to yourself: "these costs have already been made", but relate costs to an activity. When people work on a project, they make costs. You include a proportionate amount for office costs, including cleaning and servicing. No, that is not free:

if there were no project, the project areas would not require cleaning. Some companies are very good at excluding the costs of project members employed by the company from the budget: "we pay them already". Naturally, this mustn't happen; if you make use of a company's own employees, you must at least apply inter-company settlement costs and preferably fees that conform to the market. You must, as it were, isolate the costs for the project from the total costs for the company.

This form of budgeting leads to almost instant success: the estimate is so high that the project cannot be financed and can therefore not be started. Latch on to the reluctance that naturally exists within companies against spending large amounts.

And then, of course, there is the magical pound. The few pounds which can raise the costs of the project over the magical limit of, say, one million or ten million. A project costing £2,000,000 seems much more expensive than one costing just £1,950,000. Make sure your budget always exceeds the magical limit. Your client will think the difference is a lot greater than those few pounds

Let us look at other ways of using money to sabotage a project.

Long-term success through a budget downgrade
To achieve long-term success, you should make sure the estimated costs are too *low*. This allows the project to get off to a flying start because the budget was lower than anticipated. You allow problems to emerge during the course of the project, when it becomes clear that the costs are rapidly rising. By producing a budget that is far too low, the chance of exceeding it increases. As project manager, you arrangethe best time for having the project stopped. If your aim is to produce an enormous shock with a massive budget overrun, which leads to the project being stopped, you should ensure that you orchestrate things carefully and suppress the first signals of budget overrun. It could be that it is to your advantage to have the plug pulled on the project, for example, because then part of the turnover of allied construction companies has been made. In that case, you report the overrun in stages. If your client does not intervene, he becomes jointly responsible for the increasing excesses and in many cases he will give the project a lot more leeway in the hope that it will all turn out right in the end.

But you must keep one risk in mind: if you repeatedly report that the budget is being exceeded, your client's confidence in you will rapidly decline despite his involvement and he will want to replace you as project manager. Misery without action is the most probable reason your client will use for this. You should therefore ensure that every report of an overrun is accompanied by a measure that fits into your sabotage aims. The measure must give the client the idea that you are tackling the problem. You are going to analyse the problem, investigate where the cause of the problem lies, how serious the problem is and you will then offer alternatives. You shift the focus from the project to the problem, instead of to the project result. The analysis measure delays the project, increases the costs and makes no contribution to your project aim. Your sabotage objective: *'Analysis paralysis'.*

"NO PROBLEM, MORE THAN ENOUGH BUDGET!"

If you are to produce a cost estimate that is too low, you must sweep your money under the carpet. A nice effect of this is that you know exactly which cost estimates are too low. That gives you the opportunity of bringing up the actual amount required at a tactfully chosen moment. Artificially reducing the money required is something we call Budget Downgrade. There are many methods for this. In the first place, the budget can be lowered using arithmetic. The costs per hour used in the calculation can be lowered. That has an enormous impact on the bottom line. You can also reduce the costs of other calculation units, such as a square metre price, a cubic metre price and a unit price. All nice things to reveal at a favourable moment. Even better, you can generally blame the supplier.

Another thing that works well is to assume as a starting point in your documents that *many internal employees* will participate in the project. The argument is not only based on costs; it also ensures that the knowledge and experience gained is retained within the company. This would otherwise leave the building with the external consultants. But because everybody realises that the project cannot be run without additional manpower, a number of external people are then hired. This takes place in accordance with the agreed policy that stipulates a certain proportion: for example, 35% external, 65% internal. This proportion is, in most situations, far too optimistic. Every effort is made to recruit people, but in some specialist areas, the internal specialists you planned for are simply not available. They are considered indispensable by their own department. And so additional external people are hired. The consequence is that the actual expenditure on the project will be higher. There is an overrun, but we had the proper policy in place and we did our best to carry this out, but it just didn't work, for very clear reasons. You have a perfect explanation for the higher costs.

Another effective method is the *reverse project break down*: lump complex activities together, simplify them. This disguises the actual work and the costs related to it.

Finally, *limit your budget stages*. Don't budget everything, but only the first section. Enough to have set an irreversible process in motion, and ultimately enough for a magnificent cost overrun. Some refer to this as *the nose of the camel effect*: you can't tell by the nose that there's an enormous animal attached. First of all, try to get the nose through the door, and you have a good chance of success. Then the rest. Nobody thought there would be another two project humps.

"REALLY, THERE IS NOT MUCH WORK LEFT"

If you read the papers and professional literature, you will notice how many projects overspend like mad. Computerisation projects in particular are regularly stopped because the costs are soaring. But never at the beginning, always half-way through, when a lot of money has already been spent. And the argument is also familiar: we've already spent so much, there's no way back! Break the rule: the fact that so much has already been spent on a project is no reason for spending even more on it. Introduce the notion that investments must lead to return. Stand firm on the original plan, create rest and certainty. Indicate that 'we are on course', that the waves may be towering high above us, but this requires a firm hand at the wheel and we mustn't trim the sails. It is wonderful to see how jaded sailors' rhetoric still has a place in serious 21st century meetings.

Suppress the yield of the project result

The yield of a project must be related to the costs: to do that properly, a *business case* is produced. Drawing up such a business case offers perspectives for you as sabotaging project manager: the balance between costs and yield is extremely precarious.

Short-term success

For short-term success, you must estimate the yield as low as possible, so that the business case is negative. Not much is expected from the savings or extra yield. If you combine this with high operational costs for the solution that will be implemented, the business case will prove pessimistic and people won't rush to start the project.

Long-term success

For success on a longer-term, you must make a high estimate of the yield. In this way, you can justify your high costs. In the long term it will emerge that the costs were estimated fairly accurately, but that something is wrong with the yield: there isn't any.

An example to illustrate how this works: *a business process redesign project for a ministry costs £30 million spread over two years. This is based on contracting extra consultants, the design and construction of a new workflow and the licences for the software. It is an estimate which is not too low. The yield is expected in increased efficiency. A number of jobs will also disappear. The efficiency has a disadvantage: it is difficult to express in money. The client estimates that throughput time will be reduced and states that a 20% gain in efficiency must be achieved in two years. For the jobs, the assumption is that this will lead to a reduction of 100 FTE (full time equivalents). That is a saving of 100 times an average gross income of £65,000, a total of £6,500,000 per year. The client assumes that the annual savings will only come into force at the start of the second year after the end of the project. The whole investment will be recouped after just under five years. The sabotaging project manager is all too happy to stimulate these calculations. However, they are, in fact, rather difficult to achieve. The saving in FTE in two years seems very quick. Nothing has been reserved for redundancy costs, despite the fact that the departure of the FTEs will involve considerable costs. In addition, the operational costs of the new solution are not included, something which the sabotaging project manager can open to discussion at an appropriate moment.*

The business case is considered objective, but it is far from that. The result of the business case can be influenced by manipulating the costs and/or the yield. There is evidence that project saboteurs are active in this field (even without using this instructive book!).

The construction of the HSL (Hi-Speed rail Link connecting the Netherlands to the French TGV network) and the Betuwe railway line (connecting the harbour of Rotterdam directly to important German railway hubs) both ran 'slightly' over budget. At the beginning, the cost estimate was low. The reason behind this: there was considerable political pressure and a social interest in making sure the railway lines went ahead. So an optimistic estimate was made. And just look at the figures: an over-spend of £500 million is conservative.

That the construction of the railway lines went ahead is only due to the apparent need for them and the positive business case. If the project managers had budgeted the actual costs of the projects from the start, they would never have got under way.

Is the HSL an exception? Not at all. Read George Packer, affiliated to the New York Times, *author of a recent book about the war in Iraq. We read there that the cost estimates for the American Iraq operation and the reconstruction of the country were deliberately kept low in order to ensure support for the war. And then the figures: The initial budget assumed total costs of $ 2.5 billion. Detractors who suggested that it could very well prove to be more than $200 billion were brusquely swept aside. By now we know that the gargantuan amount of $200 billion was not nearly enough.*

Steer the project to its end

A sabotaging project manager must have the skill to keep out of the firing line. You must direct your sabotaging actions at factors and people who do not fall under your mandate: the client, the user, the selected supplier.

During the preparation, you ensured a vague project assignment and approval from the client of a list of requirements. Since this list of demands is the source of the project's demise, it is important that they be kept vague for as long as possible.

Your designers will soon reach the conclusion that they have a lot of questions about the requirements. They will have to meet with the users and business architects about this. They get and use the possibility of introducing new requirements, but new requirements are changes, and changes have to be budgeted afresh. The project becomes more expensive and will take longer. Stimulate this increase in requirements; whisper that the client is prepared to foot the bill. Time, money and result increasingly deviate from what the client originally agreed to. Inform the controller about what has happened and ask whether the business case is still positive. Your friend the bureaucrat will inform the client of the bad project situation for you.

" YOU DID ASK FOR A FLEXIBLE SOLUTION, DIDN'T YOU?"

The second possibility offered by a vague point of departure is to turn the matter around and give your fellow project members the freedom to take the initiative and continue the build within the scope of the vague requirements. You cordon off the project and forbid the members to discuss it with anybody outside the group. Statements such as, "I brought you in as specialist" or, "I thought you were a professional" generally have the desired effect. Your specialists will make their own choices.

One thing you must fail to do: tell the client and the user what the results will look like. A consequence of your actions will be a distrustful client. Just as you are starting to build, he has the project audited. That is not a problem. You are building according to the requirements (that can be shown), your design has been assessed internally, your approach is immaculate, as is the conclusion of the auditor. You invite the client to have the users carry out the acceptance test; after a year they will finally see the result.

With an ear-shattering explosion, the project is blown apart. The result does not meet the expectations of the client and the users. As project manager you point out that that is impossible: the system satisfies every single requirement. The users will shout: "Then the requirements were wrong". Your answer: "But you drew them up and approved them yourselves." The client is now looking for a new job.

The General Manager makes a mistake

How a project manager, thanks to clever cooperation and manipulation, can doom a project to failure in the interests of self-promotion.

The project takes place at a textile manufacturer. This medium-sized company was, in the nineties, part of a large international textile holding. The Dutch subsidiary was completely independent with its own purchasing, production and sales departments and its own staff.

The company works with an out-of-date production planning and management system. The support contracts with the suppliers of hardware and software are coming to an end and cannot be renewed. If the company wishes to survive independently, it is essential that a new planning and management system be implemented. The general manager seeks the advice of his IT manager. He asks the IT manager to advise him on the best way of solving the problem.

The financial director, however, believes he is ripe for the next step in his career. Within the current organisation, the only position that could make this possible is that of general manager. He is a friend with the IT manager outside the office; within the company, the IT manager reports directly to him. The IT manager knows his ambition and reasons that if he were to be given the position of general manager then the IT manager could possibly become financial director — a win-win situation.

The IT manager's plan is simple. If he can engineer the failure of the IT project and at the same time pin the responsibility for its failure on the general manager, there is a good chance that the management of the holding will fire the general manager. The IT manager involves the financial director in his plan. Together they concoct a scheme that would keep them both out of the firing line. In this scheme, the general director acts as client. The

IT manager advises the general manager to hire an external project manager from a major IT company to solve the problem with the support contracts. This external project manager consults with the IT manager, but reports to the general manager. The general manager views the IT manager as the client of the external project manager, but the responsibility is totally his.

The core of the undermining strategy of the IT management and the financial director is: 'Demand much for little'.

The recruited project manager's assignment is to select a standard production management software package and to implement it in the textile company. The IT manager and the financial director prepare the available budget and intentionally keep it low.

The external project manager is used to working for large companies and runs this type of project on the basis of a standard package selection approach, which he now follows rigidly. And that's why he dresses it up for all he's worth. He deploys a specialist for every knowledge area. Because of the limited budget, all he can manage is five part-time specialists for a period of four months. He lets the IT manager know that this is really not enough, but continues all the same. The IT manager assures him (orally) that additional budget will become available.

In order to create consensus for the project, the IT manager suggests creating a work group made up of the experts from the company itself. The members of this workgroup must input the company expertise and draw up the requirements. The IT manager ensures that there are experts in the group who differ in their professional opinions. The effect is obvious; the large number of external experts ensures that much time is spent in consultation. The internal experts waste much of their time in trying to convince each other. A concrete result, however, does not arise.

To prevent the project running out of time and budget, the external project manager raises the problem with the IT manager. But the IT manager has already decided which solution will prove the most controversial and advises the external project manager to choose this option, as it is the most feasible, and to submit it to the general manager for approval. The general manager adopts the proposal of the external manager and in this way takes a decision that is not supported by at least a part of the company. A number of the members of the work group throw in the towel; they still participate officially, but no longer share everything.

The production management software is ultimately chosen on the basis of half information and bad requirements. Those responsible? The external project manager and the general manager. The software proves unsuitable for its purpose and major adjustments have to be made. Slowly but surely the project begins to cost more money than original budgeted. The limited budget is exhausted.

The IT manager now asks the external project manager to produce a realistic cost estimate. With the remark that "additional budget will become available" echoing in his memory, he does a professional job and presents the actual costs. He reports to the general manager that the project will cost twice as much. This information is also passed on to the financial director by the IT manager. Initially, the general director gives the project the green light; after all, a lot of money has already gone into the project.

Some time before the finishing line, the IT manager informs the financial director and advises him to have the project audited. The financial director then reports the problem to the holding; the board decides, in compliance with his advice, to have the project audited. The auditors completely demolish both the project and its management. The general manager and the external project manager are given the blame. The IT manager and the financial director are complimented because they intervened before things went completely wrong. The general manager is relieved of his duties. The financial director temporarily assumes his position and asks the IT manager to become the interim financial director.

The new interim management declares the external IT company in default and demands the refund of a large part of the costs made. The case goes to arbitration and the IT company is ordered to refund all the costs it has received together with compensation for consequential damage. This money is used to complete the project – successfully. The interim titles quickly disappear and the two successful saboteurs are officially appointed as management of the company.

Tips for the sabotaging project manager:

- Find more than one client

- Make sure the project assignment is vague with a list of requirements that is open to differing interpretations

- Keep the project plan very general

- Select project specialists who adhere to different methodologies

- Select project members of an indifferent level

- Do not involve all interested parties in the project

- Make sure you have good informal communication channels

- Manipulate the bureaucrats with well-designed, slick reports

- Budget for either short-term or long-term project failure

- Influence the Business Case of the project result by manipulating costs and yield

- Analyse problems, but take no corrective action

- Ensure that the points of departure are under constant revision

Investigate the project manager's actions

The first step is to assess if the project manager is a sabotage risk. From the checklist in chapter 1 you can answer a few of the following questions: What happens to the project manager if the project fails? Will he lose his job, or is there a promotion in sight? Will his department be reduced by 20% because of a new IT system? Or will he be rewarded with a new job if he finishes in time? Two very different incitements, with two markedly different outcomes. In the first case, the project manager is not in a hurry. In the second he will do what he can to deliver in time.

By answering these question the intrinsic motivation will become apparent. These questions have to be followed by: if he loses his job, could he easily be employed elsewhere? And if not, are there any personal consequences like having to sell his house because of the mortgage? In other words, how is the project manager considered, as a well-trusted and accepted specialist or as a ship passing in the night?

The second step is all about the facts. Chapter 2 gives the approach to follow. Look at the facts and, very important, look if there is a pattern hiding in the facts. Do new problems pop up all the time without the old ones being solved? Does the manager consider the procedure to be more important than the result? Does he prefer formal meetings and decisions above informal decision-making? Well, if this is the case and you see a pattern (it happens regularly) you'd better beware and take appropriate measures.

Let's see what measures can be taken. As with every stakeholder, it could be quite helpful to align the personal and project interests of the project manager. So, if the project manager finishes in time delivering the right result, there must be reward waiting. That will influence his attitude towards the project.

There are several types of rewards one can think of for the project manager, eg:

- Early retirement without salary drop;

- Higher salary scale

- Financial Bonus

- Expensive training to boost his career

- Promotion

If a reward is not an option, the only way out is replacing the project manager with a project manager who does not have an interest in project failure. This might be an externally hired project manager.

But then watch out for another incentive: if the project manager is hired from a consultancy firm, he might get a bonus from his firm if more external staff is hired on the project.

BBC abandons £100m digital project

The BBC has scrapped a £98m digital production system, which its director general said had, "wasted a huge amount of licence fee payers' money".

The Digital Media Initiative was set up in 2008 but was halted in autumn 2015 having never become fully operational.

"I have serious concerns about how we managed this project," BBC director general Tony Hall said. An independent review has been launched, "to find out what went wrong and what lessons can be learned", he said.

The Digital Media Initiative (DMI) was intended to transform the way staff developed, used and shared video and audio material, and was seen as an important part of a move of resources to Salford.

The corporation said the initiative had been badly managed and outpaced by changing technology, and that to carry on would be throwing good money after bad.

Source: BBC News, 24 May 2013

'A lesson learned', indeed, but if we want a licence fee of twice £98m at least to have some revenue, we have to look at the underlying incentives. What was the goal of the 'expensive consultants'? Could this have been turnover rather than finishing the project in time? And was the staff really interested in going to Salford, or was a different incentive at stake?

6 | The sabotaging user

As the user, you often only appear in a project at a later stage — and even then in a subservient position. Completely wrong! According to the most recent insights you should be involved in a project at an early stage and you must clearly have your say on things.

This puts you in an enviable position to undermine the project. Professional literature is now describing the emancipation of users. 'We do it for the user', is what you read there. And in this way, the power that you have as user has been formalised. As undermining user, you have many opportunities for sabotaging the project.

Be unspecific about your demands

The first thing that has to be done is, of course, getting yourself into the group of core users. How? You do this by showing a healthy interest in the project with the project manager of the project and his most important consultants. Choose for this the contracted project employees; they don't know the organisation and need information. Show them that you have ideas for improvement. Pass something on, but remain modest. When somebody latches onto the idea, don't say that it came from you. Once you have done this a number of times you will see a reversal in the roles: the project employees will come to you. You have become a participant in the project and will be used as a source of knowledge.

Today's project manager will contact you for the project before it is precisely known what has to be built. As the user, you will be allowed to think about the demands which will be made on the solution. Those requirements are extremely important for the project, since every subsequent step in the project will be related to this, starting with the design and ending with the acceptance by you, the user. Step one for you, as the undermining user, is to ensure your very limited participation in drawing up the requirement. You leave all that as much as possible to the project leader and his team. Your argument is simple: they are the specialists and they know how it should be done. In IT projects in particular, these specialists have the charming habit of drawing up extremely technical requirements, which you, as the user, are totally unable to understand. The nice thing here though, is that the project leader will ask you to sign off on this set of requirements, all of which are very vague to you. There are users who do just that... but not you. You need to understand what it all means, and this is always an issue for discussion. The project manager wants to get on with things but also wants to avoid any future misery and for this would really like your approval as user.

You suggest to the project manager that you will only say yes when they have built everything because then at least you'll be able to see how it works. As far as you're concerned, the project can go ahead. But the project manager doesn't want this. He makes an attempt to perfect the list of requirements, and he really wants to involve you in this. You continue to ask for clarification and approve nothing. When, as the undermining user, you sign off on the requirements, you are a goner.

If you then, on delivery, claim that you haven't received the product you intended, the answer from the project manager will be: We built everything according to your specifications and you approved everything yourself. Often the project manager adds the friendly advice that as user you can, naturally, submit a request for change if you are not completely satisfied. A budget can be requested for this and then, perhaps, that little extra could be built.

Allow the clarification of the requirements to enter the realms of the absurd: have every single point explained, "What exactly is meant by that?" will be your habitual question.

It may take some time before a specialist has explained exactly what is intended.

When you are in discussions with a designer, give the impression that you are being exhaustive in answering any questions, but omit some essential details. You do this by delving deeply into certain unimportant subjects and, at the same time, omitting to discuss the important details.

Make sure you do not speak the same language as the designers and builders. That isn't difficult: there is a world of difference between users and technicians. Use your own jargon to counteract that of the specialists. Do everything to avoid being sent on a course with the technicians where you learn to speak each other's jargon. Even when everything has been stripped to the bone, you, as the undermining user, still do not approve anything: well, after all, you're not a nerd; you have no notion of the concept of response time. In the end, the project manager will throw in the towel and will start with non-approved requirements and ditto specifications.

Obstruct progress

The stage of design and construction now begins, but when this happens things do not come to a standstill in your world — the world of the user. That is completely normal: in the time it takes to design and to construct a project, you change your demands as a user. And you are entitled to do so; keep in mind, you still haven't approved anything. A particularly appropriate and natural moment to introduce new demands is during the testing of the new system. As user you are entitled to undertake a test and, needless to say, you come to the conclusion that the system does not in any way live up to your expectations. This brings you a totally different insight and you report this to the test coordinator who then rejects the system. It's back to the drawing board. The builder makes a new design, in line with the new requirements, and starts building again. When delivery comes round again, you are extremely pleased with the revised version, but there are just a few new things you would like. No, the system cannot be put into production unless those changes are made. The builder has no choice. He grumbles a bit, but has no alternative but to return to the drawing board. Yet again. Don't continue with the test. Instead, insist that you first want to see the change and only then can you fully assess the next piece.

As the undermining user, you have even more trumps in your hand. It is true that the builder has constantly discussed things with you, but you cannot be held responsible for all future users. A support team should have been set up to start with. And as the user, you would have been held responsible to that team. The team could also have given you a mandate. Pity that nobody thought of that... So, now such a team has to be set up. That this could be at the expense of progress is fully in line with your sabotage plan.

It could mean that as the undermining user you could become pressed for time. Obviously an estimate was made of the time you would spend on things, but you spend less time than is necessary. It all boils down to the fact that at the start of your project involvement, you were not completely clear about the time you had available. If you make yourself available to the project at no expense, most project managers will find that very attractive. What they often do not realise, however, is that it is you, rather than them, who decides when you can be deployed. As the undermining user, it is much better to have the costs borne by your own department. You can more easily give priority to the work of your own department. The project suffers and that is exactly your intention.

Manipulate communication

As the user, you generally do not have an official channel for reporting your contribution to the project. That is comforting. It means there's no need to distribute formal documents with your name on them. You can therefore limit yourself within the framework of the project to the means of communication that most efficiently frustrate a project: *gossip and innuendo.*

Sources of information

When you, as the user, wish to spread information, it is extremely important that you not be identified as the source. Therefore, do not leak any information known only to you. Your information comes from the official sources within the project, to which everybody within the project has access. The group disk or project disk generally contains the most comprehensive information about the project, from steering group minutes to management reports and memos. If information you leak can be traced to one of these common sources, there is not a cloud in the sky. Surf regularly through the project data. If you know something that is not generally known, then you must ensure, before you leak it, that this information has been formally filed under the project. A good method of achieving this is in a meeting, where you bring the point to the table. Once the minutes of the meeting have been drawn up, the time for spreading the information has arrived.

Spreading information

An excellent location for spreading information is the copier. Place a confidential document on the glass plate of the machine. You will be amazed. It is almost as if the copier handles the distribution all by itself. If, for example, you allow a document about an organisational change to lie around before it has been discussed in the Joint Consultative Committee (JCC), you will find the effect amazing: you enable the JCC to open the attack before management is fully prepared.

The most indelible impressions are not those on paper, but those made in informal contacts. The idea behind this is that people believe that only then are they hearing the truth. Even if such a conversation begins with "Just between you and me", you know as the undermining user that the content will spread like wildfire.

> *"Someone must have been telling lies about Josef K., he knew he had done nothing wrong but, one morning, he was arrested."*
>
> Franz Kafka: "The Trial", (1925)
>
> Translator: David Wyllie

Informal contacts have the advantage of not being revealing, something that cannot be said of paper proposals. Those are, after all, a formal documents and they must contain the necessary reservations. Every company has a number of places where people hang around and gossip. Smokers are now parked outside by the front door. That smoking area is an excellent place for leaking things. The other place that is particularly favoured by notorious eavesdroppers is the coffee machine. In such places you can, unlike in formal communication, titter-tatter anonymously.

Use that mechanism. Drop an anonymous remark at the coffee machine that it is very doubtful whether HR will actually support that salary administration project. Make sure there is a grain of truth in it: somebody in HR must have expressed his doubts about the salary project. Confirm that doubt but — take care — just "between you and me". That gives some guarantee that the source will remain anonymous when the rumour starts circulating.

... OFF THE RECORD

You can achieve a lot with informal contacts; people simply want to belong. They really want to feel they are part of the in-crowd, the group that always hears those snippets of news before anyone else. That is often succinctly expressed in the frequently heard complaint: Why do I never hear anything? Exactly: Because you simply don't belong. So make use of informal contacts. People are open to it.

Never underestimate how much happens 'off the record'. It is very tempting when the well-known TV presenter or radio journalist says to the person he is interviewing AFTER the mikes are switched off: "That's an interesting story but, now that the tape's off, let me ask you, OFF THE RECORD, what's the real story?" In that mood of confidentiality and driven by the yearning for prestige and wanting to belong, the person lets the cat out of the bag. Well, the tape's not running, after all. But what do we see the next day? A headline in the newspaper. This mechanism can be wonderfully misused.

The project manager often makes use of communication in order to obtain broader support for the requested change. We see that that sells the project: the story is much better than the reality. The intention is to convince opponents and doubters that the project really isn't all that bad. It is fashionable to send just about everybody a newsletter and announce to the world that the project is under way. Those newsletters generally have a very high 'we're simply the best' content. How often do they contain the phase, "currently a lot of hard work is taking place..."? That doesn't mean that hard work is actually taking place, no; the intention is to create the impression that people are working their socks off and that that is great and good! As the project saboteur, it is to your advantage to recognise this. You know that communication sugar-coats everything, and that's something you can use on the grapevine. The message usually reaches the director within the hour. The director asks the project manager for clarification, and from then on he has to confine himself to the facts, confidence is damaged, and you have created a breach in the project's fort defences.

How two social workers secretly save the organisation from making a big mistake

Local city councils used to grant subsidies to welfare institutions on the basis of permanent positions, such as social workers. The institutions were not required to account for the hours spent. The underlying idea was that the professional was best able to decide to what extent a service should be provided.

Several years ago, however, the government decided to finance the service provision of welfare institutions on a project basis. Various suppliers were given the opportunity to quote for the same care services. The city council selected which institution would be allowed to provide a specific service for a certain year. Because the subsequent service provision contract specified the hours that the service was allowed to spend, the selected suppliers were obliged to account for the hours actually spent to the city council concerned.

You can image that the social workers were not particularly happy with the new project approach and the associated monitoring.

In response to the new government policy, the board of a certain social institution decided to introduce a project hour registration and reporting system. They contracted a consultant who had previously implemented such systems for a number of architectural offices.

The government's measure was not greeted with much enthusiasm, although the board were unable to do anything about it. But the fact that the manager decided to support the measure with an automated system was met by enormous resistance. The consultant assumed that the resistance would decrease if he involved the future users in the implementation of the system. And so he actively went in search of future system users who were willing to devote themselves to the project.

Two of the older social workers, active for more than 20 years in social welfare, decided, over a cup of coffee, to block the implementation of the system: "We won't allow ourselves to monitored!" Both enjoyed, thanks to their experience, a certain standing in the organisation and they are also exactly the sort of future user that the consultant — who was also the project leader — was looking for.

The dyed-in-the-wool employees produced an ingenious plan. One of them infiltrated the project in order to become a confidant of the consultant and then manipulated the project from the inside. His colleague took on the job of influencing their colleagues. The infiltrator reported to the consultant, who eagerly included him in his project team. He complimented the infiltrator on his attitude and insight into the necessity for the project.

The saboteurs decided to point the consultant in a direction that would be totally unacceptable to the employees of the institution. Instead of pushing for a system with minimal monitoring, the infiltrator asked for maximum monitoring and registration: "The best thing would be if the system registered coffee and comfort breaks". Enthusiastically, the consultant immediately set to work on designing the system. In the meantime, the saboteur's partner kept their colleagues in the dark; resistance at this point was not what they want. The project must blow itself up when so much money has been spent that there will be no way of restarting it.

The consultant gets his design approved by the manager, largely because he indicates that the user — the infiltrator in fact — was completely behind it and therefore it is reasonable to assume there would be full support. Then they started building the system. Two programmers were contracted. The expectation was that the system would be ready for use within five months. Every social worker would then have a PC on his desk; a network would have to be set up and an administrator found: all in all, a considerable investment for a welfare organisation.

After two months, just before the investment in the infrastructure was made, the following stage of the plot is put into action. The infiltrator had, of course, kept the contact person fully up-to-date on the project. The contact person told his colleagues that he had heard that the new system won't give them any freedom at all: "Everything you do will be recorded — minute by minute. You can't even go to the toilet without accounting for yourself!" Everybody in the organisation was up in arms. The time had come for the following step. The contact person had heard that the consultant had caused so many problems in an architectural office that the company went bankrupt. The consultant actually told the infiltrator that he had once worked for a bankrupt architectural company. The causal link with the bankruptcy is made up, but there is no way to check it out. The next piece of gossip fed into the organisation is that the manager wants to use the system to check whether each social worker is operating efficiently.

The story about the quality of the consultant quickly reaches the manager's ears. Using the database of the Chamber of Commerce, the manager discovered that the architectural office concerned did indeed go bankrupt. The social workers now involve the Joint Consultative Committee (JCC). The chairman of the JCC requested a meeting with the consultant, and when he readily admitted that the intention was for the system to register every visit to the toilet, the time for action has arrived.

The manager was then confronted by the employees and the JCC. It was quite clear that they would not cooperate with this. The manager explained that the system was not meant to monitor individuals, but was just intended to simplify the reporting to the city council. Nobody, of course, believed this argument as the city council didn't require such details.

The manager reached the conclusion that it was pointless to implement a system that would not be used. Furthermore, the manager started to have less confidence in the consultant, who had not listened properly to the end users and apparently had a history of bankruptcy on his conscience. The manager was happy that he had not yet spent money on the infrastructure, the PCs for the social workers and the system administrator. That money would be reallocated for additional administrative support to help social workers with their project quotations and time registration. The plug got pulled on the project and everybody could now get on with their work in peace. Sabotage successful.

Tips for the undermining user:

- Ensure that you get involved in the project

- Do not book your own costs on the project

- Delay the process of compiling the requirements by the specialists

- Never approve the requirements in advance

- Never understand the designers and the specialists

- Ensure that new requirements are added to the project during its execution

- Frustrate the project with gossip and innuendo

Investigate the user's actions

With the stakeholder analysis described in chapter 1it is is not difficult to identify which user might not be supporting your project and to find out what makes this user tick.

Find out what happens with him when the project results get delivered, just like with the project manager. Is his department in danger? Is his job at stake? What happens to his position? Is the job less interesting because of a redesign that was introduced? What mentality has the user? Is he resistant to change? Or is he fully involved in the company's success? And is he proud to be a member of the crew?

Then see what events take place. If the user wants to slow things down, he might regularly come up with new or changed requirements. Bringing about the need for additional specifications resulting in a new design, build and test round. The user will call it progressive insight, but in fact it is progressive delay, an extremely efficient and widely used way to postpone the project. Watch out for impossible user requirements. The user tends to ask more than he needs, just to be on the safe side. Quite a large part of all delivered software, based on the agreed specs, is never used.

Does he prefer formal agreements in steering committees to a more practical approach? Or is he avoiding the formal acceptance with the argument: "I really need to see the system in operation first before I can judge if this is the right approach".

His behavior need not be condemnable. It is fully understandable that if your wife, kids and mortgage depend on your job, you want to keep it. The thing is: not to condemn the attitude, but rather understand the motive. And then find a way to deal with the situation. A way to do that is money. If, for instance, a user is delaying the project for obvious reason of possibly losing his job, what compensation is required to make him change his mind?

Early retirement? Or a fantastic training he could previously only dream of? If you think that to be expensive: think about the money you waste on a month delay in your project. It very easily takes much more money to delay the project one month than to give a retirement impetus of £100,000.

McKinsey on large scale IT projects

A McKinsey study of 5,400 large scale IT projects (projects with initial budgets greater than $15M) finds that 'the well-known problems with IT Project Management are persisting.' Among the key findings quoted from the report:

A.   17 percent of large IT projects go so badly that they can threaten the very existence of the company

B.   On average, large IT projects run 45 percent over budget and 7 percent over time, while delivering 56 percent less value than predicted

Source : McKinsey & Company in conjunction with the University of Oxford. Study on large scale IT Projects, 2012.

It is Interesting to note that 'well-known problems with IT Project Management are persisting'. If you do not address the root causes of these problems, and forget to look at the human factor, yes, the problems, although well known, will persist!

7 | The sabotaging specialist

As a specialist, you have a distinct place in a project. Whatever your role as a specialist — architect, designer, builder or administrator — you understand the solution. That knowledge is the most important weapon you can deploy against the project. If you are to be successful in undermining the project, you must know the objective of the organisation. So you must first immerse yourself in the project objective, determine what changes must be achieved, and how the project manager has designed the project to achieve them. The basis for your terror attack on the project is knowledge: use that knowledge with purpose and the project manager has no chance at all.

The specialist and his assignment

You have the line management on your side. Line managers want to ensure peace and quiet in the organisation through the predictability and repeatability of processes. They want to anchor both objectives and processes in the organisation. A project is, by definition, a fight against this anchoring. A project means change and therefore is, by definition, a threat to the line organisation. For you, as undermining specialist, this knowledge is the perfect target for your actions. If you, as the project saboteur, wish to blow up the project building with a minimum of explosives, you must make full use of the weak points in the construction. If such weaknesses are not initially present, then you deploy your knowledge and know-how to weaken the construction.

As specialist, you have, needless to say, particular knowledge about specific components. Broadly speaking we can assume that you are either a specialist in the area of the functionality of the solution, or you are a specialist in the area of the technical realisation, the construction of the functional solution. As functional specialist you respond to that which the organisation needs. As technical specialist, you translate that need into a working solution.

An example of such a functional specialist is a business architect. The business architect translates the organisational problem into a functional solution. The technical architect adds the sauce of technique to it. The first has considerable knowledge about the organisation and about defining the functional solution. The second has considerable knowledge about the technical possibilities.

In the following we use as examples the business architect and a technical architect, showing just how they can use their knowledge, know-how and position to damage a project.

Business architect

Magnify the problem

As business architect, you have considerable influence on the preparation of the project. You are one of the few people who can make an inventory of the problem and determine the demands for the solution. Nothing is simpler than to start by mapping the problem inaccurately, by making it larger or smaller than it is. The tip here is to magnify the seriousness of the problem out of all proportions. Imagine that the problem is that customers of a car dealership have to wait three days for a quotation. You could then say, for example, that more than 80% of the quotations issued do not result in the sale of a new car, while market research shows that this percentage is normally only 30%. "We are losing customers!!!!" Up to here, all well and good. The organisation has a major problem that must be solved. The extent of the problem gives you the opportunity to demand more than is necessary. "If we are to be competitive, we must be able to issue a quotation within 10 minutes," and to make it more serious still, "We must be able to offer the customer immediate financing". According to you, as a specialist, the number of quotations issued will increase enormously — and so too will the number of cars sold.

By magnifying the problem, you can greatly exaggerate the demands, that is, the requirements. The heavier the demands, the more ponderous the solution. Very quickly the point will be reached where the costs for the solution will far exceed the possibilities of the company. If management nevertheless starts the project, the excessive demands will generally result in the need to find new and expensive technologies to implement the solution. An important fact about the success of most projects is to make sure you are not the first to adopt a new technology. Flip that advice on its head. An important piece of advice for helping projects fall flat on their face: make sure you are the first.

Create gaps in the solution

The power you have as business architect over the content does not end when the project starts. Once the project is up and running, the business architect will be the person who assesses the designs. In this role it is easy to create confusion, particularly when several designers are involved. Because you are the most important supervisor, you can allow errors to arise everywhere in the design. It is amazing to see how sometimes complete sections of the design are simply forgotten. The project leader has no idea about the content and generally doesn't see that whereas the functional designer often only has one section under his control and therefore doesn't see the whole thing. And this immediately shows where you can create gaps: between the various individual design sections and the places where the design has to interface with its environment.

And when they have finally completed one section, you give your conditional approval. "Before I can approve everything, I will first have to see the rest." And if the rest is there, then you say that the design is extremely complex and you will need more time to assess it. This is the moment to show that it is full of errors. That shouldn't be too difficult because you've engineered them all yourself. Once you have found the errors, you will have lots of time to assess the rest of the design. In the meantime, you let your scepticism become clear to the organisation. A healthy distrust of the solution will naturally arise.

Never approve anything

Whatever you do, never approve or reject the design! Delay is the greatest enemy of the project. At any given moment, a project manager will choose to start the next stage of the project with a design that has not been approved. Now it's prize time! You ignore the project for a while. If questions are asked, you give no answer. Just let the project muddle on. After a while, you start asking whether sections are ready; you haven't heard anything for quite some time and you would really like to see how things look. If the project manager is not very experienced, then he has simply ploughed ahead, but there is certainly nothing that works. Now is the time for the magical words: 'Prototype'. You suggest that a part solution is used to demonstrate that the solution is really going to work. This is the moment you get the organisation behind you; they have, after all, taken a long time and we haven't seen anything yet. And at the same time you harm the project process to the quick: after all, the plan adopted only foresaw building after the design was complete. You naturally ask for the Prototype for a section that is full of gaps and that also requires considerable interaction with the environment. The more parties that are necessary for the Prototype, the smaller the chance of success. The project leader knows this as well, but he hasn't been the one in charge for quite some time. And your argument is naturally that a Prototype only makes sense for a fundamental part of the functionality.

Propose changes

As improbable as it may seem, there are still projects that survive these attacks. Fortunately, you will get more chances. During the construction you cannot do as much as the functional expert, except perhaps the odd random action about the speed of delivery. What you *can* do is propose changes. The best changes are ones that are unavoidable. For example, demands that are imposed from outside the organisation, such as the demand imposed on the banks to ensure that the identification of customers is perfectly arranged. When you bring up such a demand during the construction, the whole project can grind to a halt because people first want to investigate the consequences.

The last step where you can take control as a business architect is during the acceptance tests. Now you make use of the fact that you never approved the designs. You condemn the things that were invented by the project to the rubbish bin; you propose an alternative proper functional solution. The nice thing about a functional change is that it then has to go through all the stages of development. The project leader will often choose to allow the tests to take place; he is after a result. This, in combination with the parallel development of a new part solution leads almost by definition to configuration management problems. The development of the new solution, and the testing and repair of the old solution, get in each other's way.

Inform the internal auditors

As the thing progresses there are several other parties who would be only too willing to help you frustrate the project. A great partner is the internal audit department. This department is an off-shoot of corporate bureaucracy and sticks to the rules to an absurd degree. The audit department generally enjoys a considerable level of trust from the management of the company: its assessment can be the nail in the coffin for the project. Something that the internal auditor will typically look for is the traceability of transactions in a system. Is it possible to identify who made which transfer and when? If there is an obvious gap here, doubt about the whole development will soon arise.

Another important party who can assist you is the security department. In the internet age, security is a hot item. If there are potential security leaks in the system, no self-respecting company would ever implement it. Terms that can help you here may be 'encryption', 'external links' etc.

To summarise: as a business architect you apply the following sabotaging rules:

- Magnify the problem

- Make excessive demands

- Be incomplete

- Assess, but neither approve or reject

- Regularly propose radical changes

- Do not accept the solution

- Create vagueness in the organisation

- Involve auditors

The Technical architect

Prevent a solution that is technically possible

Another fine role is that of technical architect. You may not draw up the functional demands, but you are involved in the demands made of the technical solution. Will it be an 'Object Oriented' solution or are we deciding on the 'classic 3GL solution'? As technical architect, you contribute professional content know-how. You know what technical developments are taking place in the market. Your most important sabotage aim is to prevent the solution being feasible. The advice here is: be creative. Promote a development technology that has never been used before.. A nice approach is to select solutions for which you know there are far too few developers available. The solution may be fantastic, but you won't get any support.

As technical specialist, you also have influence on the functionality. The business architect has the demands, you have the solution; you decide what can be done. If you wish to bring the project to an early end, you must reduce the demands from the organisation to a level at which the solution no longer addresses the original problem. You do that by making use of your technical knowledge. Support simplicity; indicate that certain demands cannot be achieved for a reasonable price or within the time available. Introduce risks that nourish the fear of management of making the wrong investment. The chance that management adjusts the demands downwards is considerable. The solution may certainly be simpler, but it doesn't solve anything any more.

If people nevertheless decide to allow the project to proceed, you turn your argument around. In the literature, you found a solution that makes a lot more possible so you rework the demands into a very advanced solution making proposals against which the original, non-adapted demands pale in comparison. Your solution appears to come straight out of Star Trek.

Time for price escalation. A complex solution requires expensive specialists, the infrastructure must be expanded, other computers are required, and the development environment must be adapted. The more change, the greater the chance of misfortune. The project manager produces a new cost calculation, resulting in a solution that is considerably more expensive than the previous one.

You have introduced the following dilemma:
1. There is a good solution, but it is expensive.
2. You can build a system for a reasonable price, but that isn't really a solution.

The chance is great that people will now pull the plug on the project because they do not want a second-choice solution but do not have the money for the Star Trek solution.

Manipulate the assessors of the design

If people choose to continue on track one, then sabotage success is assured. You can deploy all your knowledge and know-how to design the most complex solution you can imagine. The larger and more detailed, the design the better. The more detail included in the design, the easier it is to leave unnoticed gaps. Most reviewers only read the first few pages of a large design; they often don't bother reviewing further. The other mistakes go undetected and are properly built into the solution, with all the consequences that entails.

During the tests, the errors will fly around the room; the result is an immense amount of repair work that cannot possibly be completed given the complexity of the solution.

Ensure monitoring

In order to create more agitation, it is nice to advise the project leader to have a code review, an inspection of the software, undertaken by an external party. Such a code review will quickly reveal the complexity of the programming and show that the chosen solution is very progressive but not sustainable. Decision-makers will pull the plug.

To summarise: as technical architect you apply the following sabotaging rules:

- Reduce the demands below the objective of the solution

- Make the solution complex, offer the possibility of increasing the level of demands

- Introduce new technologies and solution methods

- Make the design very detailed

- Be incomplete

- Have your design reviewed

- Involve auditors

The specialist, the reporting and the communication

Communication is a fantastic instrument for you as specialist. You have, of course, the formal written channels in the organisation. After all, you write reports on the designs. You use these resources to influence the content of the project. Even better are the places where you can express your opinion informally. And because you are a recognised specialist, people always take your opinion seriously. Just like the undermining user, you use the coffee machine, the smoking area or the copier for your informal messages.

"I AM CONVINCED THAT THE FOUNDATION WILL CARRY ALL THIS!"

More formal are the meetings, to which you, as the communication specialist, are always invited when things get critical. Sometimes by the project leader, sometimes by the director. There is always somebody who will use your opinion as an excuse for a decision.

There are many destructive psychological aspects to a meeting. Although this is a somewhat more formal gathering than at the coffee machine (minutes are taken, the informant is known, 'just between ourselves' has a different meaning), a meeting is decisive for the psychology of the project. If the meeting takes place in a good mood, it will support the project. Strangely enough, you can manipulate the mood through secondary factors. Things like: is the meeting room in order, am I sitting okay, are the documents accessible, have they offered that awful coffee, do they have those nice biscuits?

A meeting offers a perfect opportunity for undermining a project. When a project manager is attacked in the meeting and is unable to defend himself robustly, this damages the project. As specialist, you are at home here; after all, you were asked to attend because of your knowledge of the content. For you it is incredibly simple to raise an omission about which the project leader does not know the background. A more devious ploy is to provide the project manager with incomplete information and at the same time ensure that all the real facts are fully known by the director. The omission you reveal may have nothing to do with the actual condition of the project. If the project manager is unable to parry this in the meeting with good arguments, it will still damage the project.

A few tips on how to use the meeting to achieve your objectives:

- **Diverge and converge at the right moment.** If the meeting as a whole seems about to reach a decision, then a new issue must be raised. Mention something that hasn't yet been discussed. The meeting will eagerly debate this new issue and forget all about the consensus that had nearly been reached. The same is also true for details. If the meeting seems to be getting bogged down in details, emphasise the main line. And vice versa: if the main lines are clear, trouble the waters with details. The aim is clear: never let the meeting come to an end.

- **Turn the project manager into a scapegoat.** Suggest subtly that he was responsible. Didn't he release money before getting the approval of the steering-group?

- **Use your knowledge.** As the saboteur, you are well-informed. You understand the material better than the project manager, you understand the players in the game with all their aversions and preferences, and you know your own possibilities. You are capable, unscrupulous and motivated. Use your knowledge at the right moments; ask the project manager questions he cannot answer. The impression will emerge that the project manager is not well informed.

- Ensure that you are armed with a large number of '**words that kill**'. These are statements that can catch people off balance. For example, once plans are carefully drawn up, a term such as 'analysis paralysis' can prove highly destructive (you suggest that planning does not result in very much activity). If, on the other hand, people set out without planning first, ask for an explanation about the 'improvising results method' and request a business case.

- **Be intellectual and academic**: whenever a clear decision seems about to be taken, mention some new factor. "Yes, but how does this relate to the declining costs of the new LX 956 memory chip?" A participant at the meeting is not readily inclined to admit that he has missed the development of this chip in his professional journal. The least a meeting can do is decide that something should be reviewed. No decision should be made in this meeting, but a committee should be set up for further review. Propose appointing a few scarce professionals to the new review committee. They'll be too busy to get much done and the tempo of that committee will then not be too high.

- **Prevent** the meeting from drawing <u>conclusions</u> by pointing out the danger of an inaccurate interpretation if all the facts are not known.

- If, at long last, a conclusion is presented, ask: "do we really want this presented in such a rough state?" Then **water down** the conclusion and continue doing so until there is nothing left of it.

- Try to direct the discussion at very **general aims**. You will see that the more general they are, the more people will agree with them. Ultimately, it will become so general that its implementation will have no effect whatsoever.

- **Concentrate the discussion on the way in which the problem is approached** and not on the problem itself. That costs a lot of time!

- Introduce **comparable issues** that shroud the original issue.

- Say that **the problem is connected with another problem** (that is not difficult!) and state that the other problem must first or also be solved. That ensures that the original problem is not tackled too quickly.

- For every proposal make sure you have a **counter proposal**. Introduce it and then let everybody else decide that something between the two extremes is the best way to go. The result is a watered-down conclusion.

THE CALCULATIONS ARE TAKING FAR TOO LONG
THE COSTS ARE BECOMING ASTRONOMICAL

THAT'S BECAUSE OUR SOFTWARE IS OUT-OF-DATE. WE NEED THE LATEST VERSION!

THE NEW SOFTWARE IS TOO POWERFUL FOR OUR CURRENT COMPUTERS.

SO WE WILL JUST HAVE TO REPLACE OUR COMPUTERS.

OK. WE'll BUY NEW COMPUTERS AND SOFTWARE!?✶

WITH WHAT?

How a specialist manages to frustrate the replacement of a complex computer system by being a monopolist and specialist at the same time.

A security ministry administers a number of rapidly growing databases containing various sorts of criminal data for its investigations. These data must be absolutely confidential, extremely accessible and well secured. The day-to-day management of the data is carried out, under the responsibility of one of the departments of the ministry, by a specialised operation.

The manager of this operation receives an internal memo with the advice to expand and modernise the current system as extra functionality must be added. The IT department confirms that this is indeed desirable and recommends replacing the old system. The management knows the high demands that are made of the system and asks the IT department to start a project for preparing the replacement.

The IT department sets to work: a project manager is appointed who sets out the standard process, lists the demands and consults the departments.

The most important department that the project manager involves in the research is the department that makes use of the system that is destined to be replaced. The head of this department is recognised as the specialist in his field. He publishes on the subject in trade journals and enjoys an international reputation. He and his department have a good reputation in the world of crime fighting, based on the expertise of its employees. The new system will review a number of existing activities; it offers the possibility of making comparisons and makes use of artificial intelligence.

The head of the department has quickly drawn his conclusion: this new system will harm his reputation and knock him off his pedestal. He swiftly decides to thwart this. But he does not rush into things. If he were to shout heatedly and emotionally that he wasn't in favour of the replacement, then that would damage his professional image. He believes that he must use his own professionalism to destroy the project. He plans his sabotage with care and maps the most important stakeholders who he will have to influence: the management of the operation, the IT heads, the director-general and the influencers at the ministry. He aims his arrows at the professionalism of the IT project manager and the integrity of the systems supplier. He decides not to participate in the project group for the new system; he wants to keep a free hand and not commit himself to the project objectives.

The saboteur starts discussions with the stakeholders. Thanks to his long years of work experience in the field of crime fighting, he knows a lot of people at the ministry. He tells them that people are interfering with his department and his professional way of working: "These newfangled ideas are not good for the security of our country. And our reputation abroad is also at stake. We are thought of as an extremely reliable partner for international criminal intelligence services. We wouldn't want to damage that trust, would we? And look at the soft reputation our country has; our system shows that we are far from liberal in every area! On the contrary, we tackle crime and the current system and department contributes to that!" He also says that the new system would wipe this all out because it makes hardly any use of the enormous expertise within his department. The people he talks to do not make any commitments, but the specialist makes sure that he leaves behind the impression that things have taken a turn for the worse in crime fighting.

His next step is to make it perfectly clear that the project manager of the replacement project is simply not up to the task. He circulates articles from the trade journals, which state that other countries have not considered replacing their systems because they are still completely adequate. He subtly suggests that the IT project manager has made a miscalculation about the replacement but that you couldn't expect anything else as he is, after all, not an expert in the field. He offers to visit several foreign ministries to see what people there think of the replacement. When he returns he writes a report with a predictable conclusion: replacement is not necessary. He distributes the report to the stakeholders. The IT project manager feels forced to go on the defensive and explains that there is an assignment to investigate how to replace the system. Orders have not been placed and naturally the opinion of the specialist will also be taken into account. At the same time, the project manager emphasises the need for the new solution.

The next step of the specialist's strategy is aimed at the supplier. If the system is replaced, the supplier of the current system will most probably also supply the new system: it is, after all, a specialist matter and there are few suppliers in the market who can handle it. The specialist spreads the story that the supplier is showing monopolist tendencies, is driving up the price and naturally has an interest in having the system replaced.

In the mean time, the replacement of the old system is being prepared: a project organisation with a steering group is set up. The members of the steering group see the possibilities offered by the new system but hear that the current system can operate for a while longer. Furthermore, the specialist presents a financial review showing that the replacement is more expensive than the project group suggests.

The project group reports to the steering group and recommends replacement. It emphasises the risks in the current system, points to the functionality that the new system offers, and reiterates the demand for this functionality from the customers of the data. It is, in fact, simply an essential replacement of a critical system, concludes the report. The steering group weighs the pros and cons and decides on the replacement. The system is ordered.

The specialist clenches his teeth but persists. He reports to the highest level at the ministry, refers to his earlier conversations and states that there is something seriously wrong taking place in his department. In these talks, level skipping is rampant. The specialist has his contacts and uses them, even if he goes over the head of his boss, who, incidentally, is a member of the steering group. Doubt begins to fester at the top of the ministry. Of course there is no time to investigate things thoroughly, but the specialist-with-the-reputation can't be completely wrong, can he? And it is, after all, a critical system, and it also involves international contacts. Who will shield the minister if questions are asked in parliament? And who is responsible? People decide it is better to be safe than sorry and pose incisive questions to the head of the section to which the specialist reports. The head of the section feels obliged to take a closer look at the matter. He carefully reviews the decisions of the steering group and consults several of those involved. He hears that there is greater doubt than the decisions of the steering group would suggest. He is also concerned about the consequences of taking a wrong decision and, after careful consideration, reaches an interim decision. The order for the system is frozen in order to allow a time-out. He argues that by doing so, he is accepting his responsibility. The ministry is content with this interim decision.

But the supplier was already implementing the first part of the order and persists. Only after further consultation does he agree to stop. Half of the system has by then already been supplied, but cannot be implemented as it is because it is incomplete. It is stored in a dry place and will remain there, unemployed, for several years.

The specialist sits back and relaxes. No harm has been done. His department is unchanged, his image has grown. All in all, a successful piece of sabotage.

Investigate the specialists' actions

In most projects, specialists are involved. They might have unique knowledge that is indispensable for the project. One could easily imagine that such a specialist, like a system architect, a consultant or an accountant, is tempted to misuse this position for his personal benefit. The stakeholder analysis helps you to get an idea on the drivers of the involved specialist.

If the project succeeds, is he out of work because we then move into the maintenance phase of the system? If the project is in bad weather, will his position then rise in importance in order to help save the project? Is his knowledge indispensable or is it just that adequate documentation is lacking and we have to rely on the specialist?

The key driver of a specialist is often his involvement in the solution. If he was, for instance, the architect of the old solution, don't expect him to support a new solution he did not design.

What does his contract look like? If he is paid per hour, the incentive for delay is called turnover. Be aware of the specialist who is not willing to share his knowledge. He might have a personal reason for it. With sound distrust as an investigation tool, you might learn a lot.

Then have a look at the relevant facts: is the specialist continuously introducing new problems or is he solving existing ones? Is there a large flow of changes in specifications? Is the specialist meeting the deadlines of the project? Do his reports get in in time? And, as always, look for a pattern, a repetitive occurrence of events.

A specialist might hide behind The Method (with capitals), whether this is PRINCE2, Scrum, Component Based Development, or whatever. The Method however, should never be in the lead. The method might structure your actions a bit, fine so far, but it should never take the place of common sense. If a specialist can only justify a step by referring to The Method: beware, a saboteur might have landed. At the same time, if The Method is his only argument, you might have the wrong professional all together.

Solutions to a sabotaging specialist are never far away. His contract could be adopted in the sense that his personal stimulus fully coincides with that of the project, e.g. the bonus structure. If that is the case: a great starting point.

Involve the specialist from the beginning of the project in drawing up the new solution. If you were not able to involve an important specialist from the start of the project, provide him with an intellectually challenging assignment. In many cases, the key driver for the specialist is intellectual ownership of a solution.

Don't include specialists in your project that you don't really need. If too many specialists are involved, there is at least one who will not commit to the solution and at some point in time will switch over to the opposition.

MI5 has become the latest government organisation to add to the casualty list of Britain's failed multi-million pound IT projects

The Independent has learned that a decision by the recently departed head of MI5, Sir Jonathan Evans, to abandon a new digital records management (RM) system will cost tax payers over £90m.

The new RM system was supposed to be in place last year to help MI5 deal with the increased threat of terrorism posed by the Olympics in London. Among the added IT expertise brought in was a team of expensive consultants from Deloitte. One of its aims was to integrate intelligence data and analysis across all the Government departments that feed into MI5.

The old system was regarded as out-of-date and ill-equipped to deal with new global security threats.

Source: The Independent, 12 May 2013, James Cusick

8 | The sabotaging member of the Joint Consultative Committee

In some industries, the members of the Joint Consultative Committee (JCC)[1] must be consulted about organisational change projects. In most cases it is a legal obligation that it be consulted. The Joint Consultative Committee is therefore an excellent position for you as project saboteur.

The Joint Consultative Committee is no longer the union-like caricature of the party that constantly shouts that, "this mustn't cost jobs". The Joint Consultative Committee is mainly deployed to give substance to the idea of joint governance. The Joint Consultative Committee, and thereby the employee, is a participant in the company management game — and therefore also player on the business sabotage field.

Make friends with the director

As member of the Joint Consultative Committee, you become involved in any change project at an early stage. The director who consults you will have less than noble intentions, but these are covered in a fashionable sauce of joint responsibility. He knows that the JCC can be a force in any change project. So it is advisable to have the JCC on your side.

The director pursues the modern route: he states that he is a champion of joint decision-making and joint management. Joint responsibility is part and parcel of this and for this reason, the JCC members

---

[1] Explanatory note: When mentioning: 'Joint Consultative Committee', reference is made to any National (or Domestic) Work Council, the Employee Work Council, the Joint Working Parties Employee Forum, and the Employee Representative Forum, Labor-Management Committee (USA); under the information and Consultation of Employees Regulations (ICE), as well as to the European Work Council for Multinational Companies; under EC regulation (Council Directives 94/95/EC, 97/74/EC, 2009/38/EC.,or the Labor-Management Cooperation Act (USA 1978).

are being rightly briefed about the imminent reorganisation. The JCC members can feel flattered because they are privy to plans nobody else knows; a privileged position. What's more, they can influence the content of the decision-making. The correct response from you, as project saboteur is: create a good position for gathering information and use that information to derail the project. The wrong response is to be flattered, to show understanding for the position of the director, to become committed to the projected changes and to be less critical about the proposal.

If you are successful in undermining the project, you must, from the very start, build up a good relationship with the director. He will be all too happy to cooperate. Think of it as judo: first learn where your opponent's strengths lie. You learn that by associating yourself with him. Move with him, let yourself be moved by him, let him take the initiative and ensure that you register every move he makes. Mirror his movements. If at the start you start throwing up counter arguments, you cannot build up the desired confidential relationship and the flow of information will stagnate. Like in judo: what happens if you pull hard on the collar of your opponent? Exactly: he braces himself, he takes a broader stance and seeks a solid position, for he will not allow himself to be thrown just like that. So don't tug at the collar of the director. Don't offer immediate resistance, but wangle an invitation for a good discussion. Show understanding for the position; prove yourself a worthy conversational partner. Of course, you have also seen that there is competition from the Far East and that the salaries there are lower and that it is now all about finding the right response to this. You fully understand that the company has to invest in knowledge, that being more flexible at work is an option and that standing still is not. After a few confidential meetings, you will know the draft plans: you know that hundreds of colleagues will lose their jobs!

You use this information to prepare your resistance. You do that while at the same time retaining the excellent information position by concealing what you do with that information. The director will then continue to feed you knowledge and information. He trusts you. Then the moment arrives to think of judo again: you know what the plan entails, you know on which leg the entrepreneur will place his weight. You know the weak points of the plan. Then the planning can be disrupted simply by giving that one leg a nudge. It is a noble sport and centuries old; the rules are familiar. Don't let anybody claim it isn't fair play!

While you, as undermining JCC member, have been enjoying your special status and have been receiving information, you have naturally done some preliminary work on your sabotage plan. You have mobilised the rank and file and broadened your support. You know that the JCC will not accept such a reduction in jobs. You have had calculations prepared and drawn up an alternative plan. You use the information that you have received during the confidential stage. The plan looks good; there was enough time to work on it. It assumes different economic models and is well prepared.

When the day arrives for the company to present its plans, you naturally also take your place in front of the cameras. The question that is asked is: "And what is the reaction of the JCC to these plans?" It is a great feeling to be able to calmly open a file (press copies are available at the rear of the hall) and reveal a carefully thought-out alternative for saving the company, while retaining a great many jobs! Victory for the JCC!

Mobilise the collective
If the JCC does not enjoy a favourable information position, an alternative approach is available to you. You acquaint yourself with the plans for change and you prepare for action. Naturally there is the traditional action, varying from written protest to actions at the gate, but there are more subtle, more effective, more project-criminal approaches.

You make an analysis of the interested parties. It is probable that you, from the JCC, are not the only one with objections to the plans. There are more people who find it unpleasant that their jobs are at stake. You make an inventory, as JCC project saboteur of the interested parties and join them. It is time for the good old collective. You carefully mobilise a group of spies who will provide you with all the information you need and undertake various acts of sabotage for you.

The nice thing about a project that will cost jobs is that the project manager will need information from the very people who are under threat of losing their jobs. The specialists will have heard from the director and the project manager that an important position has been set aside for them in the new organisation. The project manager has also understood Maslow's Hierarchy of Needs (Appendix 1).

You must therefore be quick. Before the project manager has taken any steps, you must have already spoken to the specialists and explained what is about to happen. You explain that many jobs will be lost unless we do something; in fact, there's a good chance that the whole department will disappear. You explain that the project has to gain insight into the current process in order to implement the change. Management will offer some of you the chance of helping in the project and you expect that the offer will prove attractive: keeping your job or possibly, getting a better position. You next emphasise that you have seen management's plan and that there is absolutely no room for the retention of all jobs. You quote examples of companies that have undergone a similar process: in the end, everybody had to leave. And the collaborators were unable to find a new job anywhere!

When the management makes its proposal — and rest assured that will happen — nobody will fall for it: "I'm not going to cooperate in my own downfall".

Ensure procedural mistakes in the request for advice

You have formed your team; now it is time for action. If the project has already started, then you cause delay. At a given moment, management will submit the plan to the JCC for the obligatory formal request for advice; before taking the next step, the JCC will have to issue an opinion. There are a number of simple directives that are applicable to a request for advice. A request for advice must contain information about the motives behind the change, together with the consequences for the personnel and measures to alleviate these consequences. In addition, the request must be submitted in writing and in time so that the JCC can have its say in the decision-making process. In many cases, the management deliberately ignores these rules; be on the alert for that. When that happens, you start a procedure that paralyses the process to such an extent that the project has to be sent back to the drawing-board. If, in such a case, you have an alternative plan, the company will often accept that in gratitude. In other words: mission accomplished!

Manipulate the solution outside the parameters of the Request for Advice

If you can't trip up the project through the process, then you will have to concentrate on the content. That is more difficult. After all, the company has employed a large and important consultancy firm to substantiate the proposal. You haven't got the money for that. How on earth can you manage to torpedo the advice of such a respected consultancy? You can make a small sally at the content by involving the trade union; they have specialists who can assess the content. You mustn't spend too much time on this stage; you seldom win a fight with these top consultants. Fortunately, these consultants generally bow out when the project actually begins. The attack you prepare is aimed at the feasibility of the project. For this, you mobilise several users whom you know are against the project. You help them find favour with the project manager and advise them on how to prevent the project reaching an accepted result. It is important that your partners in crime introduce changes that cause an impact on the Request for Advice. The nice thing here is that, when the project manager decides to adopt these changes, he has to go to the JCC again. He may have done that the first time; the second time is generally overlooked. You wait before intervening until the change has become an integral part of the solution. The project will then be stopped with huge negative financial consequences.

Keep calm and the line won't break

How the chairman of the Joint Consultative Committee was able to obstruct a ministerial policy line for years on end.

In the year 2000, the European Union decided to give the development of knowledge in Europe a strong push.

One of the consequences was that some national universities and colleges had to align their curricula. For this reason, the boards of the university and three colleges arranged a meeting in 2002 with the intention of forming a project group. The most important objectives were the harmonisation of the study curricula and a management and staff merger between the various institutions.

The Joint Consultative Committee is not informed about the collaboration and the proposed organisational model until several months after the discussions between the various boards have taken place. The chairman of the JCC of the university immediately sees the spectre of this merger; it will cost a lot of jobs. One institution will, after all, only require one support staff and one JCC. The chairman of the JCC is fully aware that he cannot and may not block the collaboration on content; this is, after all, stipulated by the government pursuant to the European decision. In his approach, the proposed staff merger must be thwarted. He works out a strategy of gradual implementation delay. As chairman of the JCC, he continues to pull the sabotage strings. When the proposal from the Supervisory Board is discussed in the JCC, the chairman (in his role as saboteur) explains that the JCC's involvement occurred late in the project and, according to him, more time is needed to study the proposal and review the consequences. To keep the supervisory board on a leash, the JCC states that in principle it does not object to cooperation with the colleges in the region but does require more time. The supervisory board does not want to ruffle the JCC's feathers and agrees to postpone the decision-making.

The saboteur convinces the members of the JCC that it would be best if the collaboration plan is implemented in small steps. He also emphasises that a management and staff merger is not desirable; after all, the objective of the university education is not the same as that of the colleges. Merging the various institutions would not be to the good of the academic level of the university. And this would mean that the objective of knowledge improvement would not be achieved. At the beginning of 2003, the JCC presents an opinion to the Supervisory Board, which excludes all elements of a merger but praises the collaboration. The JCC produces a step plan, in which each step must be approved by the JCC. The Supervisory Board, which thinks that the process has taken enough time already, agrees with the opinion of the JCC in the hope of saving time. The supervisory board produces a step plan providing for a number of subsidiary plans, which will be implemented consecutively.

In compliance with the proposal from the JCC, the content side of the collaboration is first investigated. For this, five subject-oriented steering groups are formed, with specialists from both the university and the colleges. The JCC refuses, at the instigation of the chairman, to participate in these steering groups; the council could otherwise lose its independence. The managerial web around the collaboration now begins to assume dramatic forms.

Each individual steering group must validate its subsidiary plans and content proposals with both the supervisory board and the JCC. The saboteur ensures that every proposal that contains a hint of organisational simplification is rejected. The chairman has the law on JCCs behind him; such proposals do not only require an advice, but also the approval of the JCC.

The steering groups cannot get a step further and are completely at a loss. What can they do now? Through his channels of information, the chairman of the JCC has learned that the ministry has increased its pressure on the supervisory board. The minister wants results; otherwise measures will be implemented.

The chairman wants to avoid this and realises that the image of a JCC that only blocks things is not very favourable. He must avoid people taking a different route, where he will no longer be able to execute his plan of sabotage.

In an intensive meeting with the members of the JCC, the chairman takes an important step. He reports what he has heard from The Hague (the ministry) and proposes that the JCC take a first step to bring the stalemate to an end. He still does not want a staff merger but suggests that he is extremely impressed by the skill of the steering groups, which have presented good ideas about how the content of the courses could be aligned. These study-oriented solutions can, as far as he is concerned, enjoy the full support of the JCC . He proposes advising the supervisory board to appoint the steering groups as structural organs for the study-oriented collaboration. And to make them responsible for the content of the bachelor and master programmes, as well as for the alignment of these programmes between the colleges and the university. The great advantage of this solution is that there are no negative consequences for staffing; in fact, an additional five faculty departments have been created, which must all be sufficiently staffed. Each institute maintains its own board and its own staff, with these five overlapping faculty departments. The JCC is in complete agreement with the chairman's proposal.

The steering groups are very positive about the proposal. Their important project function is thus turned into a structural responsibility. The supervisory board is also pleased with the proposal; it will allow a year-long process to be finally brought to a conclusion and the ministry can be informed about the success of the collaboration. The steering groups set to work energetically and, in just a short time, set up the curricula. The chairman of the JCC is the hero of the day; after all, a process that has dragged on for years has, thanks to his brilliant innovative proposal, achieved a successful result, which is approved by the JCC and the supervisory board at the end of 2005.

The saboteur has thus succeeded in delaying a change process for three years, has safeguarded his interests and has ultimately left the scene of battle a hero.

To summarise: as member of the Joint Consultative Committee, you should apply the following rules of sabotage:

- Gain favour with the principal of the project;

- Prepare an alternative proposal;

- Form a collective group of opponents;

- Prepare your fighters;

- Use and stimulate procedural errors in the request for advice;

- Manipulate the content of the solution outside the parameters of the request for advice.

Investigate the employee representative's actions

Again the stakeholder assessment in chapter 1 will help to identify the manipulating employee representative. For the manipulating employee representative, first you have to investigate if he acts on behalf of the Joint Consultative Committee (JCC) or if his undermining acts are serving his personal interest. This is easy to determine: execute the stakeholder analysis twice, once for his role as member of the JCC and once for his personal project involvement. The outcome might surprise you! Here we assume that he is acting on behalf of the committee.

Find out what happens to the number of jobs in the company if the project succeeds. And equally important: what happens to the jobs if the project stops or gets a huge delay? What has been the JCC's policy so far with regard to job reduction? What is the

JCC's reputation when it comes to openness and fairness? Has there always been an open dialogue with the CEO? Have a look at the influence of the JCC in the company. Has it always been relevant or just marginal? Are the representatives considered to be professionals and well informed? Is the JCC key player in an informal employee network in the organisation or are the members structurally avoided by the employees?

Then execute the Manipulation Facts Analyses. Does the employee representative always point out the formal arrangements of his position? Does he delay decision making purely because formalities have to be followed? Is there a pattern of moving items from today's agenda to tomorrow's?

In solving this, there is one option that will never work, regardless of the legal construct: that is to ignore the wishes of the employees and their representative. It is unethical or politically undesirable to begin with, but more importantly, it simply doesn't help you at all. If you want to deal with sabotage from this side, the most important step is to know the real interests of your opponents. So, check what is really behind the ideas of the employee representative.

To clarify this: if in meetings your saboteur is always stressing the importance of the procedure, is always asking for official reports and official standpoints of the company management, and is always inventing a new problem once you found a solution for the previous one, then it is time to look behind the scenes. Procedures will not be his or hers truly primary focus. What makes this person tick? And once this is clear, you can see if the real demand can be met. If done seriously, it will stop the procedural approach and a cooperative attitude comes within reach. In the end, the interest of the company is the interest of the employees and vice versa. Closing down the sabotage operation is what everyone wants, isn't it?

Of course, if you put an emphasis on politically correct behaviour, there is nothing against ensuring a better organised influence of the workers in your companies. After all the exploitation of workers is long behind us. Yes, we will grant the employees more influence, a common thing, done in many civilized countries in the world. No surprise the National Works Council Directive saw the light in 2002 in the UK. Just a sensible thing to do, right?

Well, two interest groups showed a slight reluctance. Of course the employers officially agreed with the idea, and, of course, the unions were all too happy to see more influence going to the employees. But, hold on, what happens to the decision making speed in the companies? And what happens to the influence of the unions? Not a very favourable picture all together, is it? If I, as a director of a company, have to invest in a faraway country, can we wait until the national works council agrees? Just go and tell the competition, they might like that. And how about the Union? Shall we ask them to postpone decision making until the council has made up its mind?

So, although traditionally divided, the two parties here had a common interest. The goal was politically fine, but there was no harm in postponing the paradise a bit! In consultations it was suggested that the implementation time would be 3 years (2002-2005). No need to rush into things. Adding to this relative speed was a second option: gradual implementation. Companies with 150 employees or more would have a deadline on April 2005, with 100 or more: April 2007, and 50 or more: 2008. By the way, statistics show that almost 97% of the firms in the UK employ less than 50 employees.*

To make the impact of the regulation even smaller, it was decided to have first, second and third class agreements: ranging from voluntary, negotiated and to default. It would be an interesting calculation to find out how many companies were in the last category.

The conclusion is that ICE regulations, although politically quite correct, were gradually slowed down in implementation. There also is a clear watering down of the rules. Might have been exactly what both parties involved had in mind. Other factors played a role as well, of course, like apathy among the employees. But that is passive. Being a true saboteur, action is required, and that is what happened here with employers and unions.

As PLC Thomas Reuters, Legal UK & Ireland 33 says:
"In fact, employers have flexibility to establish consultation arrangements under those regulations that are neither works councils nor national in scope, but the term 'national works council' conveniently distinguishes these arrangements from European Works Councils and from the ad hoc information and consultation obligations which arise under other UK legislation."

* Source: White & Case Europe LLP, Transatlantic Employment Issues, June 2006.

9 | The criminal conspiracy

In the previous chapters, the various saboteurs were discussed individually. The question was, for example, what you, as director, could do to disrupt the project and what you could do as project manager. There's nothing at all wrong with this, individuals can sabotage the project, but the effect can be greater still if forces are combined! If you find a co-conspirator, the effect is not simply a sum of the two saboteurs, but is multiplied. Collaboration strengths the effect so that the whole is greater than the sum of its parts. In other words: the strength of the collective.

If such a secret society is to be set up, there always has to be somebody who takes the initiative. Such a person must be extremely circumspect when searching for co-conspirators. How do you find them? Whom do you need and whom can you do without? Whom can you trust and whom should you distrust? The more people involved, the greater the chance of exposure. Searching for a suitable partner in crime is not without risk.

"WELCOME GENTLEMEN, YOU WERE HIGHLY RECOMMENDED BY MY PROJECT LEADER!"

You need an incisive insight into the power relationships within the organisation when putting together your terrorist cell and selecting your target. Who really has the power? What is their political agenda? Who is part of the bureaucracy? Who are the protagonists and who are the antagonists? When making your preparations you determine whom you can influence and how, and who would choose your side in your subversive activities.

Conspiracy and politics

It is important that you, as project saboteur, understand something of the political game. If you are to undermine a project, you must become politically active. You must join the circle of 'power and manipulation'. The term 'politics' is well known in every organisation. People understand that it is less tangible, but still very important. The term is often used to provide a general explanation of the unexplainable. One could imagine discussions such as: "Tell me why that project has been stopped and why Ahmed is not in charge of it?" "It's politics; I don't know either." It becomes worse and less tangible when people start talking of *higher* politics. That is a level above smokers' corner gossip and office machinations. It's politics in rarefied air and thus proves an even more powerful explanation.

Politics is the game of power and thus for you, as a project saboteur, an important tool with which you can exert influence in the company. That starts with a good analysis of the players. You analyse the players in the selected line-up, but also the people behind the scenes. You can easily trace the selected line-up: their names are in the project plan; they have been announced. But who has the real power? Who really pulls the strings? As the project saboteur, you track down these people. Use your political nous. Look at the company's future plans. What is going to happen in the long term? Will there be a shift in the company's core activities? Which divisions have been recently spun off? Which divisions complain about a shortage of money? Which divisions are investing? You can easily find this out informally, at the coffee machine and in the smokers' corner. Sometimes there are formal sources: take a look at the five-year plans and the annual reports issued to shareholders. What do the figures mean? Analyse how much money is invested in a division in year one and compare that to year two. Also look at the number of staff. You should be able to identify a trend. And the mood of the times can also help you here: there is a general consensus that things are developing fast *at the moment*. Use that to your advantage: for the changes and the trends that you want to see will happen sooner.

Externally, you can make use of the Internet. That covers everything: analytical consultancies specialise in collecting trend information. That is exactly what you want: trends. Predict the movement of shares: will there be gains or losses in the sector? You can derive political information from all of this. If a sector is performing badly, you will better understand why a project is stopped.

You will also better understand why a bad project manager is assigned to a large project. The background could be that it is not particularly important for the project to prove successful. Politics! And *higher* politics come into play if a manager is assigned to it whose career needs it. A clear indication: two birds with one stone.

You now know which parts of the company are in favour and those where a bitter wind blows. This information gives you insight into which players are rising stars and which are falling. This knowledge is essential to you as a project saboteur because it allows you to connect with the real people of power and, at the same time, to identify your partners in crime.

Conspiracy in a bureaucracy

Many companies are bureaucracies or have characteristics of such. It is a tried and efficient form of collaboration. Sabotage largely takes place in a bureaucratic environment. In a conspiracy, it is sensible to realise that you are thus mainly undermining the bureaucracy.

An important principle to remember is that a bureaucracy rewards people for not taking wrong actions and not for doing the right things. That means that during the conspiracy, reporting should continue un-abated; there must be a constant flow of information, which reaches the appropriate people. The flow of reports is uninterrupted and that in itself is a cause for trust. This is really fantastic and actually goes so far that a bad but correct reporting is generally well received. Exaggerated? By no means: just look at the reception given to an exception report. The report pinpoints everything that is not going according to plan: the delay, the extra hours. That is annoying but everything is impeccably reported. It gives the impression that everything is under control — despite the delay. Such cosmetics disguise the problem; there is a delay and there is a cause. But that is not what the report says. The report is made to appease the need of the bureaucracy; it reduces complexity while providing the illusion of order and control. The conspirators ensure that there is order in the reporting of the project, while at the same time they work together with all their might to block it.

It is obvious that an organisation that is organised in a less bureaucratic fashion and thus allows greater flexibility is less vulnerable to sabotage. Take this into account when choosing the area you want to undermine. There is, therefore, every reason to view with considerable distrust any newfangled idea that could lead to a more flexible organisation. It could render bureaucratic sabotage less effective.

Many bureaucracies divorce thinking from doing. Thinking is done by the staff; the line does the doing. This provides a very clear starting-point for sabotage. To start with, it takes a while before thinking reaches doing and vice versa. This means that there is a delayed reaction to any faults that may arise. Interventions are made too late. Furthermore, this shows the advantage of conspiring together: the sabotage team has representatives of both thinking and doing. For example, we see the specialist seated beside the project manager. The specialist thinks about the how, the aim of the project; the project manager supervises the execution of it. Thinking and doing are integrated. This improves the quality of the decisions and also, naturally, the speed. In such a way you can easily triumph over the bureaucracy.

Maximising resistance to the project by effective manipulation

The foundation for successfully sabotaging projects is the effective manipulation of the right people in the organisation. If you are to do this, you must understand what drives these people and what they consider important, and what their position is at the moment that you start your manipulating. A good basis for making people susceptible to suggestion is to encourage anxiety. When anxious, every person naturally looks for something to grasp on to. If you remove the thing they grasp, they will search for new values. And, as a project saboteur, you assist them in this. Most projects are started because of a need to change and this implies changing the thing to which people grasp. As a project saboteur, you use this temporary void to form your team and to manipulate the other people involved.

Effective duos

When you want to set up a sabotage team, you must first find suitable candidates. In this book, we have discussed five categories of saboteurs: project managers, directors, users, specialists and Joint Consultative Committee members. Most can collaborate with the others, but not every combination is equally plausible or equally strong.

- The combination of **director** and **project manager** is not very plausible, but it is extremely effective. If neither the director nor the executor is willing, the project will most probably not start at all.

- If the **project manager** forms a kongsi with a **specialist**, you have a team able to destroy the project both in content and in management. The most effective team arises when the specialist is a confidant of the director, and this specialist does not come from the project organisation. The project manager and the specialist can manipulate the director from two sides. The specialist can, as a confidant, stimulate certain aversions and preferences in the director. The project manager can steer the project in the corresponding direction. When both play the game cleverly, they steer the project under the guidance and responsibility of the director directly into destruction. The director will not realise who has stabbed him in the back and how it was possible that things could go so wrong.

- A similarly strong, if not stronger, duo is formed by the **director** and the **specialist**. The specialist is often highly flattered if he is approached by the director to throw his lot in with him. Any initiative by the specialist towards the director is not probable because of the hierarchical superiority of the director over the specialist. Here too the undermining action should come from two sides. The specialist must take a place on the project and from his position provide the project manager with as much misinformation as possible. In addition, the specialist is the eavesdropper who knows what takes place on the work floor; he provides the undermining director with an unending stream of information that the project manager would rather keep to himself. A fine example of a specialist who cooperates with the director is the architect. An architect is generally both dogmatic and creative at the same time. The architect generally lives on a higher and more abstract level than his fellow human beings.

You could, as the director, employ the following strategy to allow an architect who is sympathetic to you to infiltrate a project. You allow the project to proceed for a while with an architect from a particular school. This architect has an overview of everything and knows the direction being taken. After a while, you replace this architect; you claim it is absolutely essential that he concentrates on a different project. An alternate architect joins the team; he has a completely different dogmatic background. A generic characteristic of architects is that they suffer from the 'not invented here' syndrome. The replacement architect has not yet been able to exercise his creativity and he will certainly want to impress his mark on the project. Result: 'embedded change'.

The second architect becomes the director's partner in crime. After all, the whole project stinks and he is determined to do his utmost to prevent the company making an ass of itself. There are many fine, partly academic questions that the director can pose. Are the developments really aligned with the architecture? Have the long-term effects been taken into account? Is the application under construction sustainable? And for what costs? Is the solution safe? Every question triggers a creative process in the architect and an irresistible urge to change something. The undermining architect assesses the situation and then indicates that he is not at all satisfied with the solution. Consequence: put the project on hold, a decision the director can now take. To quote the words that Shakespeare penned for Lady Macbeth: "Look like the innocent flower, but be the serpent under it".

- The undermining **project manager** can secure the collaboration of the **Joint Consultative Committee**. That is not as easy as it is with the specialist: there are potentially more members who have to be persuaded. Furthermore, there is the likelihood that these will include people who have an above-average commitment to principles and who are not prepared to collaborate. What's more, members of the Joint Consultative Committee have a healthy distrust of a project manager who makes too many advances. But if this group can be persuaded, the result is a strong combination: the project has virtually no chance of success.

- The **project manager** and the **user** are not natural allies. The project manager has the reputation of not always giving the user what he wants. In addition, the user will generally not be in favour of change. But if an alliance can be forged, the combination will be extremely powerful. Unlike the alliance with the specialist, which targets the content of the solution, here the target is the acceptance of the solution. If the undermining project manager is able to manipulate the users, he erodes the foundation for the acceptance of the result. The project will then in all probability not reach the finishing line. The undermining user and the undermining project manager make grateful use of each other's information. The project manager leaks information that will lead to heated discussions among the users. The aim is to get them to take to the barricades. The director who is not prepared to compromise in the face of a mass revolution among the users is a rare beast indeed. Are you beginning to understand why so few projects actually succeed?

- A very natural and therefore very strong combination is that of the member of the **Joint Consultative Committee** and the **user**. The JCC is, after all, the organ that represents the employees (and that includes the user) in the company. They speak each other's language, and have a similar perspective: What does the project mean for the user? In this situation, the user should infiltrate the project and pass on all secret project information to the Joint Consultative Committee.

The following table shows the most probable combinations of saboteurs:

	Director	Project manager	User	Specialist	Member JCC
Director colludes with		-	+	++	-
Project manager colludes with	-		+	++	-
User colludes with	+	+	++	+	++
Specialist colludes with	++	++	+	+	+
Member JCC colludes with	-	-	++	+	+

Effective undermining teams can, of course, comprise more than two conspirators. That can take place on the cusp of thinking and doing in the organisation. Ideal combinations are:

- **project manager, user** and **specialist**. This combination of management, acceptance and content is simply invincible.

- **user, Joint Consultative Committee** and **specialist**. It is an alliance at the basis. Management (project manager, director) is isolated. In official communication, everything continues as normal with meetings are held and work undertaken on the project. But the undercurrent is clear: a breach has been made. And there is no way of closing it. This is often physically reinforced by the management: their status demands that they sit in a separate office. There is already a communications gap because of the difference in status, but if basis and management are in different offices, approaches become more difficult. It is better if the management really is upstairs — on the 17th floor, for example. You have to have a reason to go up there, otherwise you don't. That interferes with informal communications and that is useful. You can also make use of this distance for accusing management of an ivory tower mentality: they are really far from reality and thus are unaware of what really takes place down there. It's not just that they no longer have their feet on the ground but they also have their heads in the clouds. And that is all too easily associated with arrogance.

In practice

Collaboration only becomes truly effective when the available weapons are shrewdly deployed. Polarisation is a wonderful weapon of mass manipulation. You may assume that, as the project saboteurs, you regularly attend a project meeting. If, as the undermining specialist, you have convinced the project manager of a specific solution, you inform your undermining partner — for example, the user — of the weak points in the solution. Uproar in the following meeting, when the user demolishes the solution. The project manager, who is still convinced about the solution, has no choice other than to have the solution assessed. Result: delay.

In addition to encouraging differences, a further strategy that the conspirators can adopt, is structuring incidents. If the same problem is reported from two totally different corners of the organisation, this will always lead to a reaction from the organisation. If, for example, both the architect and his undermining ally from the infrastructure department report that the proposed solution does not satisfy safety norms, then hardly any further proof is needed to convince management that this is indeed the case and encourage them to take the necessary measures.

Unity breeds power

How the user, the specialist and the member of the Joint Consultative Committee form a powerful alliance to reverse the irreversible.

A department of a financial company does a lot of routine work. The department consists of 200 people. They process large numbers of requests and can hardly stay on top of the work. Delays are inevitable. The departments that are supplied are not always satisfied. Many people have also noticed that the department does not always make use of the most efficient processes. Management decides to start a computerisation project, which will result in the demise of the majority of the manual labour.

Yet not everybody is happy with this. Right from the start, the interests are divided over two groups: the director and the project leader on the one side, and the users, several specialists who fully understand the work process, and a member of the Joint Consultative Committee on the other. The classic divide becomes clear: a division between those who must implement the change and those who could become victims of it.

When the start of the computerisation project is announced, the seed of sabotage is sown. The victims decide to offer resistance. Several end-users take the lead. With the saying, 'unity breeds power' in mind, they contact one of the specialists. The users, represented by the department manager, hold a meeting with the specialist. The position of the users is under threat because computerisation will cost jobs. The position of the specialist is under threat because he is an expert in the field about to be decimated. At their very first meeting they decide to undermine the project together.

The tactics they agree are based on a two-pronged attack. In the first place, the processes that they execute will be presented as far more complicated and complex than they really are.

The specialist, who is expert in work process analysis, is in an excellent position to support this. In the second place there is the day-to-day work: many customers wait on the results from the department and they consider it a high priority that there is little or no time wasted on the project. It then transpires that it is not difficult to convince a member of the Joint Consultative Committee of the importance of the continued existence of the department. If people will have to leave, then there must be a very good redundancy scheme.

The project leader sets the computerisation project in motion. He follows the traditional rules for system development and starts with a process analysis. Because the current system is very poorly documented, he and his people have to consult with the users. These make handy use of the dependence of the project members on them. As agreed, they suggest that the process is exceptionally complex; it consists of little more than exceptions and that is why the processes require such a long throughput time. The project members analyse the process and consult with the department process specialist. He adds fuel to the flames: it is all highly complicated and furthermore, crucial to the company. Many questions cannot be answered using simple computerisation criteria but demand a professional assessment. By people. In this way, they create the idea of a process that cannot be computerised, or only at exorbitant expense.

The project concludes the first stage way behind schedule, and provides no basis whatsoever for continuation. The conspirators end the first part of the match 1-0 ahead.

Based on the advice of the project manager, the director decides to hire a renowned organisational advice consultancy firm to vet the work processes. That consultancy goes to work very strictly with a highly prescribed method of work. The users see a chance to conceal a number of things, but they are not quite as successful as before. The consultancy discovers that a few sub-departments intentionally delay the work process in order to conceal the fact that they could easily have everything done before lunch. At half-time, the score is 1-1.

The director decides on two actions: the process will be revised without it being computerised, so that immediate cost-savings can be implemented by discharging redundant staff. In addition, the project can go ahead with restructuring, subsequently computerising the work process.

The project leader sets to work again, but neglects to take something into account. The attitude of the users has changed but is now legitimate. It is like a wasp's nest that has been disturbed: total unrest. Cooperate with a process analysis that will lead to further redundancies? Not on your life! A lengthy battle ensues, during which the project manager tries to complete the analysis. The users withdraw all cooperation because they now have a valid argument: "You don't really expect us to work on a project after all those redundancies? There simply isn't any time for that." The project leader makes no progress. The score is now 1-2 to the users.

The project leader now deploys heavier artillery and asks the director for permission to implement a standard solution. He has the idea that that would work well: the work in the department is by no means as specialised as people think.

The circumstances for the director, however, have changed: his annual targets stipulate that he must achieve a certain percentage of savings on this department. It seems that he will already be well on the way to meeting those targets thanks to the redundancies implemented at the suggestion of the organisational consultancy. The pressure to turn the department upside down has receded. Furthermore, the Joint Consultative Committee has clearly indicated that further pruning of the department would be undesirable.

The director, however, is fully aware that there is plenty of room for improvement and, taking this into consideration, decides that the project should continue. But carefully and without too many drastic measures.

The project leader accepts his defeat and sets the project in motion once more and tries to improve the processes. The users and the specialist have little time for him and the project falls way behind schedule.

After the year, the project leader says farewell to the project and it is 1-3 for the users. Thanks to their structured strategy, they have been able to head off most of the intended changes; the department can return to its former peaceful existence.

Tips for conspiracy:

- Determine how the political forces are arrayed in the organisation

- List which departments are in a good position and which are less fortunate in the long-term plans and make use of it

- Make an inventory of the workings of the bureaucratic machine. Proper use creates the appearance of reliability

- Work as saboteur together with a co-conspirator. The effect is much greater than the simple sum of individual efforts

- Choose your co-conspirators with care on the basis of an overview of interests and influence

- Analyse the position of the players in and around the project and use their position and influence for successful manipulation

- Work together

How to break an alliance

It is a well-known fact that saboteurs hide behind good intentions. They do not go about advertising their true motives and making themselves known. This also applies to the alliances that saboteurs might forge. You need to be aware of these alliances; it is our experience that a project saboteur is seldom able to fully destroy a project without the help of others. The first step in finding out if alliances exist is to investigate if more than just one saboteur is active in your project. Here you follow the approach described in the previous chapters. The next step is to investigate whether saboteurs conspire. The table 'combinations of saboteurs', as discussed earlier in this chapter, is a good starting point for this investigation. Focus your analysis on the groups of saboteurs that show a high teaming probability. To investigate if these sabotage teams exist you can use the Conspiracy Facts Analyses below. First tag the possible alliances that might exist. Check if and which conspiracy observation applies to your project. And finally break the alliances.

Step 1: Identify the possible alliances

	Likely alliances								
	Director – User	Director – Specialist	Project manager – User	Project manager – Specialist	User – Member of the JCC	User – User	Specialist – User	Specialist – Specialist	Specialist – Member of the JCC
Possible alliances (Y/N)	Y/N	Y/N	Y/N	Y/N	Y/N	Y/N	Y/N	Y/N	Y/N

Step 2: Identify actual alliances

Category	Conspiracy Incident	Probability of occurrence (Y/N)								
Information	Do the saboteurs provide content for the same management reports? Eg. an architect provides information on the acceptance of designs. The acceptance in formation is (mis)interpreted by the manipulative project manager.									
	Do the saboteurs provide information for communication briefings? Eg. the director explains that the goal of the project is getting the organisation on top of the market in applied ICT. The specialist explains in the same meeting the advanced technological path to follow. Both confirm the feasibility of this path, although you know that the internal staff is not up to speed and no training plans are foreseen.									
Meetings	Do the saboteurs frequently attend the same informal gatherings (Eg. coffee machine, lunch walks, smoking area, etc.) and do they spend significant time-sharing their project opinion with their colleagues?									
	Do the saboteurs seem to avoid each other in meetings, but still show consistent behaviour? This is typically a conspiracy signal. Eg. when you receive a confirmation by a third person like: "Yesterday in the board meeting John said the same". This shared opinion might not be a coincidence.									
	Do the same people fail to attend at the same (crucial) meetings (eg. steering board)? This strategy is often used to delay or reconsider decisions (concerning design, process, etc.) because an important attendee was not present in the meeting.									
Reactions on general events	Do the saboteurs react equally on reprehensible behaviour? Do they share opinions on that matter in meetings regularly? Is there is a similarity in the argumentation? Eg. A proposal presented in a meeting is ridiculed by one of the specialists attending this meeting. The director confirms that it seems a bad proposal and sends the initiator back to the drawing board. The result of such an action often is that the initiator is frustrated and will not attempt to come with a new proposal.									
	Do the saboteurs react similarly on incidents? Eg. do they want to ignore incidents or are they overreacting to a relatively small incident?									
	Do the saboteurs question the same things all the time? That could be a sign of a delay tactic.									

137

		Likely alliances								
Possible alliances (Y/N)		Director – User	Director – Specialist	Project manager – User	Project manager – Specialist	User – Member of the JCC	User – User	Specialist – User	Specialist – Specialist	Specialist – Member of the JCC
		Y/N	Y/N	Y/N	Y/N	Y/N	Y/N	Y/N	Y/N	Y/N
Reations on general events	Do they regularly present the same conflicting opinions leading to additional analysis work instead of solutions? This strategy is often found at content level. Eg. When two specialists or a user and a specialist present a difference of opinion in a meeting, management most of the time will decide to investigate the matter further. Seldom is the question raised why this difference of opinion has not been solved before the meeting.									
	Do two or more participants hide behind "Air Bag Language (might, just about, for the time being, conservatively, as a concept, don't nail me down on this one, etc.) and is this accepted without taking a firm position? That might be a sign of wanting to conceal things. This is an often used strategy to be able to reconsider decisions in the future. Whenever management accepts this, consider that this might be deliberate.									
	Do the saboteurs deny the relevance of stakeholders? Eg. Important stakeholders are not involved in the project. This is often a collaboration between management and a specialist or management and a user. The specialist clarifies why a stakeholder is not important, this is confirmed by management thus preparing future stakeholder issues.									
	Do the saboteurs involve a large number of non-relevant stakeholders? Involvement of too many people will most of the time result in discussing irrelevant subjects, thus leading to an indistinct project foundation.									
Reaction on HR events	Do the saboteurs together regularly support or initiate proposals that logically will lead to the departure of crucial (and supportive) team members or stake holders? Eg. by promotion or de-motion of the same member of the team or making your team member crucial for another key project.									
Reaction on project control	Do saboteurs react in a similar way on audit reports? Most of the time audit reports show the standard fail factors of a project and seldom address the human factor. Saboteurs tend to react to these reports in a supportive way. Eg. if the report suggests that the quality of the staff is insufficient they support or even suggest the measure to replace this staff. Or if the report suggests that the financial plan of the project should be revised, they will certainly support that gesture (the next step would be to address the overrun that will logically follow).									

138

	Likely alliances								
Possible alliances (Y/N)	Director – User	Director – Specialist	Project manager – User	Project manager – Specialist	User – Member of the JCC	User – User	Specialist – User	Specialist – Specialist	Specialist – Member of the JCC
	Y/N	Y/N	Y/N	Y/N	Y/N	Y/N	Y/N	Y/N	Y/N

Reation on project control									
Are the saboteurs frustrating the review and approval process constantly? Eg. by withholding approvals (often used arguments are: I don't have time for review; I need to see the bigger picture first; did Mr. J already approve it?). When a director supports this argument, it might be that they collaborate against the project.									
Do the saboteurs stimulate and confirm each other to be indistinct on business cases? (eg. they add text like a high number of customers complaining, or the system is at the end of its life cycle without further explanation in the Business Case. Indistinct business cases often form the basis for changes that consume a huge amount of time. Many of these changes are cancelled because they do not make sense thus causing delay and deviating attention from the core goal a project.									
Do they ask for investigation actions regularly? In this case the cooperating saboteurs tend to alternate the role of initiating and confirming investigations. The real professional saboteurs, to avoid suspicion, even challenge each other once in a while.									
Is there a similarity in the reaction on official reporting and early warnings, dashboards, analysis, etc.? On the one hand, saboteurs tend to amplify minor issues that are reported (eg. a minor overrun that can easily be justified will be a reason to initiate further investigation). On the other hand, real issues will be played down or even ridiculed (e.g. the project manager has a problem in hiring a required specialist, the saboteur will react with a sentence like, "with your network that can't be a problem").									
Is there a shared academic approach (as in "not practical")? The common sabotage action is defending the opposite of what the project is doing. For a well-controlled project they will state something like "be practical". For a more agile project they will stress detailed configuration management and project control.									

Fill in a 'Y' in each cell for a conspiracy incident that regularly occurs in your project. The dark grey cells refer to the incidents most likely to occur for the applicable alliances. In your specific alliance, you might put the tick elsewhere, depending on your assessment. The approach gives you an indication in what direction to look for your conspiring opponents.

If you tag 3 or more 'Y's in a column, our advice is to take action to break the likely alliance.

139

Step 3: Break the actual alliances

The golden rule to break an alliance is to weaken it. Most of the time such an alliance consists of a leader and one or more followers. The leader is always the most difficult person to convert. So focus you attention at the followers. Once you have converted the followers, the leader remains. But like a general without an army, a saboteur-leader without followers will have more difficulty in harming your project.

To convert the followers, the ways we discussed in the previous chapters are at your disposal. So, start with defining the interests of the people involved, investigate their activities and find alternative ways to meet their demands.

10 | Summing up the Saboteur

In the world of project management literature there is no lack of 'how to' books. How to manage your projects to deliver outstanding results, how to manage project opportunities and risks, how to manage multiple projects and many more. Not to mention: The Twenty-Five Most Common Problems in Leadership and How Jesus Solved Them.

The one thing these books have in common is a rather technocratic approach, a strong belief in a pliable world and a simultaneous lack of taking the human factor into account. Their basic idea is that perfect planning is perfectly possible; just list out a proper plan and steer. Reality will follow your plan. If anything goes wrong, the plan is to blame. You must have made a wrong estimation, is the common reasoning. The emphasis lies with clearly following the milestones and making an exception report if something goes wrong. You all know this recipe.

Interesting enough, auditors very often follow this approach. Have you noticed that they usually list the following reasons for a project to fail: bad planning, wrong budget, scope creep, lack of resources and wrong staffing? We always wonder why the actual, the real reasons for project failure, are not investigated. WHY is the planning not ok? WHY is the budget insufficient? WHY did the scope change during the project? And WHY could the right staff not be found? We know it is not easy to leave the well-trodden path, but as stated before, only when we leave the well-trodden path we do see things that remain hidden from others: the real reasons why projects fail.

The idea of this book, basically, is that the human factor has to be considered seriously to provide an answer to this question. A major reason for project failure is to be found in the personal interest of the people involved in the project. If their interest is not in line with the goal of the project, it seems logical they will resist that goal. Yes, they might perform sabotage and manipulation activities. They come up with the wrong plan, the wrong budget and inadequate staffing, thus causing the project to fail.

In order to make you aware of the endless opportunities to undermine a project this 'how to' book shows you the steps a saboteur will follow to effectively sabotage a project. It provides you with the techniques to effectively sabotage a project. Dangerous? Not at all. It will help you understand the motivation of the saboteur and it will enable you to prevent or stop sabotage, in order to be more successful.

Based on considerable experience, we suggest many ways to change the outcome or even kill the project. The first and foremost idea is that you will henceforth learn to understand the mechanism, in order to be able to take appropriate measures. It will make you see how a saboteur, although looking very innocent and supportive, executes his destructive actions. After you read the book you should have gained a sound touch of distrust. 'Sound' because you can exaggerate mistrust leading to paranoia. On the other hand, having too little mistrust is simply being naive. We would advocate adding this human factor approach to the regular project control tools. It will make project management far more successful.

After all it can't be that hard to understand our own species: ask yourself what the human drivers are and act accordingly. The way to success lies ahead of you.

You see, a very ethical approach!

Appendix A: Suggested Reading List

For those who want more information on how to sabotage or how to stop it.

Title	Author	Publishing info
Project Saboteur and PRINCE2	Jeroen Gietema and Dion Kotteman Bert Hedeman	Van Haren, 2011 Claret Press, 2016
Execution: The Discipline of Getting Things Done	Larry Bossidy & Ram Charan	Crown Business; 1st edition June 15, 2002
Managing Corporate Change	Klaus Doppler en Christoph Lauterburg	Springer Verlag Berlin 2001
The Goal	Goldratt	North River Press; 2nd Revised edition, May 1992
Key Management Models	Steven ten Have, Wouter ten Have	Prentice Hall 2003
Psychology	F F O Holzhauer and J J R van Minden	Stenfert Kroese 1978
The Social Psychology of Organizations	D Katz and R L Kahn	New York, John Wiley & sons, 1978
The Leader on the Couch	Manfred Kets de Vries	Wiley, 2006
The Prince	N Machiavelli	
Managing Successful Projects with Prince2	Office of Government Commerce	The Stationary Office ISBN 0-11-330891-4
Organisational Behavior and Performance	A D Szilagyi en M J Wallace	Santa Monica, Goodyear, 1980
The Way of the Rat: A Survival Guide to Office Politics	Joep P M Schrijvers	Cyan Books (13 Jul 2004)
Op weg naar een Lerende Organisatie (Towards a Learning Organisation)	J Swieringa, A F M Wierdsma,	Wolters-Noordhoff B V 2003

Appendix B: Maslow's hierarchy of needs and the motives of the project saboteur

1. Physical needs for shelter, food, drink, clothes and sex. If, as a result of a project, your income were to drop so dramatically that you would no longer be able to provide for your most basic needs, then you would oppose the project with all means at your disposal. After all, somebody is depriving you of the possibility to live.

2. Need for security. If a reorganisation could threaten your job, then your security is at stake. This is a typical problem that you face with outsourcing: 'Who can tell me that I won't, in turn, be kicked out on the street in three years?' Change almost always undermines the feeling of security. The promise of a new security cannot simply replace the old security. So you see no alternative but to resist the change.

3. Need for acceptance. If you belong to a group of colleagues that bolster your primal need to belong then you feel like you are in a warm bath; you don't want to get out because it feels so good. When the threat arises that you could, through a reorganisation, no longer belong to this group, you feel threatened, even if you can continue to work within the same company. At the moment that a group of colleagues threatens to be broken up, the whole group often rebels, or a leader mobilises the group to fight against the project. You could be that leader.

4. Need for recognition. If your position as the expert threatens to disappear because of a project, then you are likely to dig in your heels. At this ego-strengthening level, you operate as an expert. Your colleagues value your knowledge and know-how. That feeds a part of you that nothing else can.

5. Need for self-development. If you are one of the innovators of the organisation and your function is under threat, you will certainly come into action. Your possibilities for mobilising people and convincing them of the disastrous choice for the project are virtually unlimited. Thanks to your creativity, there's almost no way to beat you.

Appendix C: The Agile way of sabotage

In February 2001, in three days, 17 specialists (they call themselves the 'Agile alliance') drew up the Manifesto for Agile Software development.

Manifesto for Agile Software Development

We are uncovering better ways of developing software by doing it and helping others do it. Through this work we have come to value:

Individuals and interactions over processes and tools

Working software over comprehensive documentation

Customer collaboration over contract negotiation

Responding to change over following a plan

That is, while there is value in the items on the right, we value the items on the left more.

Source: http://www.agilemanifesto.org

When they all went home after their retreat they couldn't have imagined the huge impact their manifesto would have on the world of software development. By 2015, it is clear that Agile software development had conquered the world. If you're not a certified Scrum Master, or a certified Product Owner, or if you don't understand the principles of continuous delivery, you will no longer be a game player.

There is much that is good in Scrum, in DevOps, in Continuous delivery and Extreme programming. But it also offers a host of new opportunities for the project saboteur.

To understand the Agile Sabotage potential, we focus on Scrum. With Scrum the project manager left the software development arena. Where the product owner was once wholly responsible for the requirements, software development became a team responsibility. The motto of the

Three Musketeers applies: 'All for One, One for All'. So the team doesn't float around rudderless, the role of Scrum Master has been introduced. The Scrum Master can be seen as a coach and a facilitator, he is not responsible for the team result.

It is not our goal to write a 'How to' book about Agile or Scrum. Our objective is to address the vulnerabilities of Agile development concerning the human factor.

Agile manipulating change

In our advice concerning Agile manipulating change we will stick to the three Scrum Roles:

- Product Owner

- Scrum master

- The development team

The Product Owner single-handedly determines the requirements, the priorities, and accepts the results. He then has to negotiate with other product owners to be in sync with the overall change strategy. The Product Owner combines the roles of director, specialist, user and project manager in one person. Because of this, he also inherits all the Sabotage possibilities.

Life for the manipulating Product Owner is easy. His role provides him the opportunity to:

- Deviate from the business strategy. The development team only validates if it is possible to deliver the change, it is not responsible to validate if the right question has been asked. As a result the team will develop working products that meet the Product Owner's requirements, but those products will not fulfil the need of the organisation. When will this be noticed? Probably never! Who should notice it? Who is responsible for the added value of each requirement (backlog item)? The Product Owner!

- Ensure that the results of several Scrum teams are not in sync. This is easily arranged by setting the right priorities to keep the different scrum teams in sync, while taking care that the user stories are of insufficient detail for the development team. The development team in that case will automatically select other backlog items to develop (probably of less importance and not in sync with other teams, thus causing delay).

- The Scrum Master is the authority on Scrum, although he is not responsible for the development result. From his authority it is easy for the undermining Scrum Master to manipulate the development team:

- Influence the number of items to develop in a sprint;

- Influence which product backlog items are being added to the sprint backlog by just asking the right questions. The development team will come to the conclusion that the user story is not detailed enough;

- The Scrum Master is responsible for ensuring that everyone understands what has to be delivered, or 'The definition of done'. How easy is it to secretly apply a definition of not done: just leave something out or give your own manipulative interpretation.

Finally there is the development team. A group of developers without one responsible leader. The complete team is responsible for the end result and the result supplied by each team member. One saboteur regularly expressing a different opinion is quite visible. The better sabotage approach is to organise a (sub) team to avoid delivering the results that fit the organisation best. If two or three people within the development team form an alliance they can easily manipulate the less important user stories to be selected from the product backlog or with the more important user stories, just keep asking for more detail, thereby avoiding their development.

To set the anchor point for the Agile way of Sabotage see the manifesto below:

Manifesto for Agile Manipulating Software Development

We are uncovering manipulative ways of developing software by sabotaging it and helping others undermining it. Through this work we have come to value:

Individuals and manipulation over processes and tools

Undocumented Software over testable results

Customer manipulation over customer collaboration

Responding to change over delivering results

That is, while there is value in the items on the right, the saboteurs value the items on the left more.

Statement for Agile avoiding sabotaging Software Development

The Agile approach to change will help but it's no Holy Grail to avoid project sabotage.

Therefore we propose to extend the Agile manifesto with what we have come to value:

Understand and reward the human needs over repressive measures.